AN AMERICAN DREAM

My family in Holland in 1957

An American Dream

My Immigrant Journey of Gratitude and Belonging

HENRY A. MULDER

With Martin Jumbam

Maple Books

Maple Books
An Imprint of Spears Media Press LLC
21699 E. Quincy Ave, Unit F #167
Aurora, CO 80015
United States of America

First Published in the United States of America in 2026 by Maple Books
www.spearsbooks.org
info@spearsmedia.com
Information on this title: https://spearsbooks.org/product/an-american-dream/

Maple Books and the Maple Books colophon are trademarks of Spears Media
Press LLC.

Publisher's Cataloging-in-Publication Data
Names: Mulder, Henry, 1937– author.
Title: An American dream : my immigrant journey of gratitude and belonging
/ Henry Mulder.
Description: 188 pages ; 22 cm.
Identifiers: ISBN 978-1-957296-76-0 (paperback)
Subjects: LCSH: Mulder, Henry, 1937– | Dutch Americans—California—
San Mateo County—Biography. | Immigrants—United States—Biography. |
Floriculture—California—San Mateo County—History. | Salvadorans—United
States—Biography. | Intercultural marriage—United States. | California—
Biography. | LCGFT: Biographies.
Classification: LCC CT275.M85 A3 2025 | DDC 920.073—dc23

Designed and typeset by Spears Media Press LLC
Cover design: D. Kambem

Contents

CHAPTER 1

Childhood Memories

* * *

I don't know how my parents met, but they lived about an hour's bicycle ride from each other. They were married in 1936, and a year later, I came into the world on April 8, 1937. Both sets of my grandparents (paternal and maternal) were wooden shoemakers, a craft that no longer exists. I never met my paternal grandfather, who died at age 56, before I was born.

It always struck me as a curious coincidence that my arrival into the world so closely coincided with my paternal grandfather's departure from it. Though I never knew him, I often wondered about the kind of man he was—what his voice sounded like, whether he had a sense of humor, if he was proud of the work he did with his hands. The wooden shoes my grandparents crafted were not only a source of income but also a symbol of the hard, honest labor that defined that generation. In many ways, I felt connected to my paternal grandfather through the stories my father shared and the legacy of craftsmanship passed down in our family. His absence was a quiet presence in our home, and even though I never sat on his knee or heard his laugh, I grew up with a sense of respect for the life he led and the role he played in shaping our family's history.

My Parents

My father's name was Hendricus Mulder, but he was commonly known as Hein. My mother's name was Henrica, but she was known as Riek. My maternal grandparents had a small farm beside their house where they grew food—mainly potatoes and vegetables—to feed the family. Whatever little money they had, came from the wooden-shoe business. They also grew a lot of food to feed the animals in winter.

My father worked at a meat-packaging plant. He didn't do the actual slaughtering, but he packed the meat. Even though he worked there, he didn't receive any privileges, like getting meat at a discount. He brought home ribs and bones from which my mother made soup. Since there wasn't much money available, especially during the war, we were grateful for what he could bring home.

Despite the limitations, my parents never complained. My father was a quiet, dependable man who took pride in providing for us, even when it meant long hours and little reward. My mother, on the other hand, was practical and endlessly inventive in the kitchen—she could turn the simplest ingredients into nourishing meals. The soup she made from the bones and ribs wasn't just food; it was warmth, care, and ingenuity in a bowl. We rarely had meat in the way people enjoy it today, such as barbecue and other luxuries. Still, we ate together every evening, and that ritual gave us a sense of normalcy and comfort. Those modest meals became cherished moments, reminders of our family's strength and the love that held us together through lean times.

When my father couldn't afford meat, he began breeding rabbits. As children, we had to feed the rabbits with grass from the roadside, which my father considered public property. My father would slaughter the rabbits and prepare them for sale. With the money from that sale, he would then buy a nice piece of meat for all of us.

Breeding rabbits became a family effort, and although it wasn't always pleasant work, we all understood how important it was. Feeding them scraps from the garden or kitchen became part of our daily chores, and we took turns cleaning out their pens. It was just one of the many ways our family adapted to make ends meet.

A Growing Family

I was the eldest of seven children, three boys and four girls. My brother, Teun, was born a year and a half after me. He was followed by Jan, who, in turn, was followed by four sisters: Toos, Gerda, Riekie, and Betsy. With so many of us under one roof, life was rarely quiet, and personal space was almost nonexistent—but there was always a sense of closeness and shared responsibility.

All nine of us shared one toilet, with no running water or electricity. We had no problem sharing this toilet because no one wanted to stay in there for long. Just enough time to do whatever you needed to do, and then we were out to give room to someone else. We helped each other, fought occasionally as siblings do, but always knew we were in it together. Our parents worked hard, and we children learned early what it meant to contribute our share, no matter how small, to ensure that all went well at home.

Births at Home

All seven of us were born in the same modest house that we grew up in. Three boys were born before the war, and four girls were born during and after the war. It was more than a home—it was the place where every chapter of our lives began. Whenever our mother was about to give birth, my father would quietly step out and return with a midwife, often an older woman from the community who had helped deliver many babies over the years. Hospitals were never part of the equation; that simply wasn't how things were done back then, especially for families like ours. Childbirth took place right there in the house, surrounded by familiar walls and familiar hands. It was the way of life at the time—simple, natural, and deeply rooted in tradition.

Strangely enough, as children, we never seemed to notice when our mother was expecting. Perhaps it was her quiet strength or the way daily life kept us so occupied. We were never told she was pregnant, and it never occurred to us to ask. Then, without warning, the rhythm of the day would change. Women—neighbors, aunts, or family friends—would arrive at our home and usher us children out, speaking in hushed tones and busying themselves with preparations. We didn't fully understand what was happening, but we sensed something important was underway.

When we were finally allowed back into the house, it was as if we had stepped into a new world. The air felt different—quieter, gentler. And then we'd hear it: the unmistakable cry of a newborn baby. That sound, fragile yet powerful, announced the arrival of a new sibling. It was in those moments, standing there wide-eyed and curious, that we grasped what had happened. Without fanfare, another life had joined our family, and our little house had somehow made room for more love.

War Years and Hardship

I vividly remember how incredibly hard life was during the Second World War years. Everything was scarce—food, warmth, and certainly money. My parents struggled to make ends meet, and luxuries like new clothes were simply out of reach. As the eldest child, I was the only one who occasionally received new clothes, but even those were few and far between. We were all growing rapidly, and in our household, clothes had to serve multiple lifetimes. When I outgrew something, it would be passed down to my younger brother. Once he outgrew it, the same garment would go to the next child. It wasn't uncommon to see clothes that had been mended several times, worn thin at the elbows or knees, yet still holding together enough for another round of use.

To help support the family, my mother did what she could. She bought fabric which she used to sew shirts and other clothing items for all of us. As times were hard for everyone, she became a tireless seamstress, constantly darning socks, patching holes, and sewing torn seams. Each article of clothing told a story of resilience, stitched together by her worn hands.

Winter Cold

I was in charge of the lamps, filling them with kerosene each evening before it got dark. In the wintertime, it was tough to go down into the cellar to get the potatoes using a small portable kerosene lamp. Winter was perhaps the most difficult season of all. The cold was relentless, and our home could be bitterly cold. My father, already earning very little, had to spend almost half of his salary just to buy coal to keep us warm. Even then, it was never enough. I remember the particular desperation of the time when coal became completely unavailable. We had no choice but to gather and burn wood—whatever we could find. The warmth was barely sufficient, but it was all we had. It was a time of quiet endurance, of finding ways to survive when every resource was stretched to its limit.

I remember a particular time that truly captured the desperation of those years. My father couldn't even afford to buy wood for the fire—something so basic, yet so vital for cooking and staying warm. Instead, he found a way through sheer determination. He purchased tree stumps, still deeply embedded in the ground. With nothing but simple tools and his own strength, he dug them out, roots and all. Those stubborn stumps became our firewood, feeding the flames that cooked our meals and heated our home. It was far from ideal, but it was all we had—and it was enough to get us through another cold stretch.

Large Family, One House

You can only begin to imagine the challenges of living under one roof with a large family—my parents and their seven children. We weren't just short on resources; we were short on space. Our home was a one-bedroom house on a small piece of land my father managed to buy before he got married. The bedroom belonged to our parents, as was customary, while the rest of us made do with the living room. Every evening, we would unroll thin mattresses on the floor, creating a patchwork of bedding across the room. Come morning, we folded them up and stacked them neatly in one corner, making space for the day's routines.

Despite the overcrowding and hardship, we endured. We survived five long years of war living like this—sharing everything, sacrificing comfort, and holding on to each other for strength. It wasn't easy, but it taught us resilience. In that little house, with its single bedroom and makeshift warmth, we learned the meaning of family, of resourcefulness, and of enduring hardship together.

A Foundation of Faith

My parents were devout Catholics, and their faith was not just something they practiced—it was the foundation of our entire family life. From the moment we entered the world, our spiritual journey began. In keeping with tradition, each of us was baptized two days after birth, our parents ensuring that we were welcomed into the faith without delay. The Church was as much a part of our upbringing as the walls of our home.

Faith ran strong in our extended family, too. One of my mother's sisters chose a religious life and became a nun, dedicating herself completely to prayer, service, and contemplation. On my father's side, one of his brothers became a religious brother, serving in the Church with equal devotion. Their vocations inspired great respect in our household and served as quiet, powerful examples of how a life rooted in faith could take many forms.

Sundays were especially important. We all attended Mass dressed in our best clothes and bicycling to church with a quiet sense of reverence and routine. During the week, we attended daily Mass at school, which further deepened our connection to the faith. Religion wasn't confined to a single day—it was the backdrop of our lives, present in every moment.

Even after I left home to begin working and started a new chapter of my life, I continued to live in households steeped in the same Catholic values. Whether by choice or by fate, I always found myself among families who shared the same faith and practiced it with sincerity. That continuity allowed my spiritual life to remain strong and unbroken. No matter where I went, I carried with me the firm grounding of my Catholic upbringing—a faith nurtured since birth and quietly shaping the person I was becoming.

Early Education

I began kindergarten at the age of five at a school run by Catholic nuns, which was the customary practice in those days. When I turned seven, I transitioned to a Catholic elementary school where we attended Mass every morning before making the short walk to our classrooms.

Education was entirely free during this period, including public schools, Catholic institutions and schools operated by private individuals or other religious denominations. This universal accessibility was made possible by the Dutch government's subsidy of all educational institutions, ensuring that every child could receive quality schooling regardless of their family's financial circumstances. We never had homework and never carried any books with us to school or home. All books remained in school as they were school property.

Dedicated Teachers

The kindergarten section of our school was administered by Catholic nuns who served as both our educators and spiritual guides. These women were truly remarkable teachers who demonstrated unwavering dedication to their calling. Their commitment to their students was so complete that they seemed to maintain perfect attendance—I cannot recall a single instance of having a substitute teacher throughout my time there. This extraordinary reliability spoke volumes about how seriously these nuns regarded their educational mission and their responsibility to provide consistent, quality instruction to every student in their care. The teachers in second through eighth grade were all male and always dressed in suits, which made us students really respect them. We only knew them by their last names. Amazingly, the teachers were always present. I can't remember ever having a day with a substitute teacher.

CHAPTER 2

The Invasion of Holland

* * *

The Second World War began for us when the Germans invaded the Netherlands on May 10, 1940. That morning is etched in my memory, every detail preserved with startling clarity. I can still visualize my father returning from work at approximately 9:30 AM, much earlier than usual, his face grave with the weight of terrible news as he announced, "The war has broken out!" I can still hear the tremor of anxiety in his voice. The fear in his eyes was unmistakable—a raw, undisguised terror that I had never seen before. These powerful emotions spread through our household like wildfire, affecting even us children, who couldn't fully comprehend the magnitude of what was unfolding but instinctively understood that our world had fundamentally changed.

My mother urged my father to hurry to the local stores to gather whatever supplies he could for our family. However, his efforts yielded little; the shelves had already been stripped nearly bare by other anxious residents with the same idea. Among the few items he managed to purchase was paper tape, which could be used to secure all the glass windows in our home. However, towards the end of the war, and despite my father's efforts to secure the windows, severe bombardment shattered all the glass windows into pieces.

Once the German armies rolled across the Dutch border, the Dutch military mounted a courageous but ultimately doomed resistance, managing to hold back the invading forces for three grueling days. However, when the Luftwaffe (German Air Force) mercilessly bombed the major port city of Rotterdam, reducing much of its historic center to rubble, and then issued chilling threats to subject Amsterdam to the same devastating fate, the Dutch command faced an impossible choice. To prevent further civilian casualties and the wholesale destruction of the nation's cultural heart, the Dutch army was forced to capitulate on May 15, 1940.

This surrender marked a tragic turning point in Dutch history. In just five days, Holland ceased to exist as a sovereign nation, its independence extinguished and its proud democratic traditions suspended indefinitely. For the next five long years—from 1940 to 1945—Holland became an occupied territory, its population systematically subdued, exploited, and brutalized under the harsh rule of Nazi Germany.

Human Faces of War

Many of the German regular soldiers were ordinary people just like us. They didn't like the war either. Some of them even came over to my uncle's house to play cards in the evenings.

They would occasionally take out their wallets and show us pictures of their families, whom they missed a lot. Some of the soldiers even came to church on Sundays and stood at the back during Mass. During the war, there was no tobacco, so people started growing their own. One of my uncles built a wooden machine he used to slice tobacco. Without electricity, he invented a system for generating electricity using a bicycle's wheels.

There was no coffee either, and people used a variety of corn called sorghum, which they ground and then added chicory to it, and it tasted good. People called it a surrogate. Given the limited supply of goods, the government issued distribution coupons to buy necessities for the home, particularly food. Nothing could be bought without those coupons.

Disrupted Education

The occupation profoundly disrupted every aspect of daily life, including education. For a significant portion of those five years, my siblings and I remained at home because schools had simply ceased to function normally. The educational system, like so many other institutions, had been dismantled or co-opted by the occupying forces.

During the initial years of occupation, life maintained a deceptive semblance of normalcy. While restrictions and shortages were increasingly evident, the full weight of Nazi oppression had not yet descended upon every aspect of civilian life. However, this fragile routine was completely shattered in 1944, when the war entered its most desperate phase for the German military.

It was then that German forces requisitioned our school building, transforming the institution that had once nurtured young minds into a military facility. They converted the playground and classrooms where children had once played and learned into a vehicle depot where they repaired their vehicles and other military equipment. Portions of the building were re-purposed as repair workshops, with the sounds of hammering and engine repairs replacing the voices of teachers and students. The symbolic destruction was as devastating as the practical one—our center of learning had become an instrument of war.

The soldiers were hungry and would occasionally ask us to bring them food. We brought them eggs, and they gave us some tools from their repair shop: wrenches, screwdrivers and more. They exchanged tools for food, especially as the war intensified and the Allied Forces closed in. Those tools didn't belong to them, but desperation makes people do things they normally wouldn't consider.

Living Through Occupation and Liberation

I was three years old when the occupation began, and I lived through the entire five-year period until the Allied Forces finally liberated our region. The liberation of Holland unfolded in stages across sectors: American forces liberated the southern provinces following the D-Day invasion, British forces took control of the western regions, and Canadian troops liberated the eastern part of the country, where my family and I lived.

When the Allied forces advanced northward from the beaches of Normandy, they liberated Paris, fought the Battle of the Bulge in Belgium, and reached the major rivers in the Netherlands. The Germans had heavily fortified areas around the major rivers—the Rhine, the Waal, and the Maas. To continue to advance, General Montgomery devised a daring plan, called "Operation Market Garden," involving the dropping of parachutists behind enemy lines. Over 30 thousand parachutists and equipment were dropped near the town of Arnhem. Our town lay only about ten miles from the scene of this operation, close enough that we could witness some of the dramatic events unfolding in the distance.

I still have haunting memories of watching the 101st Airborne and British paratroopers descending from the sky, their parachutes creating an almost surreal canopy against the war-torn landscape. Tragically, many of these brave soldiers were shot down before they could even reach the ground, their parachutes becoming death shrouds as German anti-aircraft fire found its targets. Despite the extraordinary courage and effort invested, "Operation Market Garden" ultimately failed to achieve its objectives. The bridge at Arnhem proved to be, as history would later characterize it, "A Bridge Too Far." Consequently, we remained under German occupation for seven additional months. Those ten miles separating Arnhem from my hometown, Twello, felt like an insurmountable chasm between captivity and freedom.

Our Home Becomes Enemy Headquarters

Six months after "Operation Market Garden," Allied Forces closed in from all directions. In early 1945, the German occupiers became increasingly desperate and erratic in their behavior. The growing pressure of impending defeat manifested itself in their frantic search for secure command positions, which ultimately led them to requisition our family home as a regional military headquarters on April 7, 1945.

The transformation was both swift and overwhelming. German officers arrived in force—stern-faced men whose heavy military boots echoed ominously through our house. They came armed with rifles and pistols, but more significantly, they carried enormous tactical maps that revealed the scope of their military operations. These detailed charts were either spread across our dining room table, covering the surface where our family had shared countless meals, or tacked directly onto our living room walls, obscuring family photographs and turning our intimate spaces into sterile command centers. The presence of these maps told a story of mounting desperation. They showed troop movements, supply routes, defensive positions, and retreat routes—clear evidence that the German military was no longer planning offensive operations but was instead managing an increasingly chaotic withdrawal from occupied territories.

Signs of German Desperation

By this late stage of the war, the German military was clearly in desperate straits. Their transportation capabilities had been so severely compromised that they had reverted to horse-drawn wagons and carriages, which they stationed throughout our backyard, as if it were a scene from a previous century. This stark contrast between their sophisticated communication equipment inside and their primitive transportation outside served as a powerful symbol of how close the Third Reich was to complete collapse. The same evening of April 7, 1945—just weeks before Germany's final surrender—the German forces hastily packed their equipment and evacuated our home, leaving behind a house that bore the scars of military occupation.

I saw the first V-1 rockets developed by the Germans. They sent them to London, flying over our house. They appeared like big fireballs flying over our homes and heading for London.

There were also the V-2 rockets, but those were shot from areas south of us.

Throughout 1944, as the Allied noose tightened around German positions, the British Royal Air Force intensified their bombing campaigns in areas surrounding our town. These strategic air strikes were designed to flush German forces from their entrenched positions and disrupt their supply lines, but they also created a constant atmosphere of terror for civilian populations caught in the crossfire.

We quickly developed an acute sensitivity to aircraft sounds, learning to distinguish between the drone of Allied bombers and the whine of German fighters. The moment we detected the approach of any aircraft, we would immediately seek shelter, never knowing whether the planes overhead carried bombs intended for German targets or if we might simply be in the wrong place at the wrong time.

When we were working or playing in the open fields around our town, we maintained a state of constant vigilance, our ears perpetually tuned to the skies above. At the first sound of approaching engines, we would throw ourselves into the nearest drainage ditch, pressing our bodies against the earth as bombs exploded in the distance. Even when the targets were miles away, we had learned that deadly shrapnel could travel far beyond the immediate blast zone, turning even distant explosions into potential threats to anyone caught in the open. These harrowing experiences taught us that survival often depended on split-second reactions and an almost animal-like awareness of our surroundings—skills that no child should ever need to develop.

I was about to turn eight years old, and as the German soldiers hurriedly packed their belongings to evacuate our home, my mother mentioned to them that the following day would be my birthday. Despite the chaos of their retreat and the fact that we were technically their enemies, one soldier paused in his preparations to give me a small package of rye crackers as a birthday gift. It was a moment of unexpected humanity amid the brutality of war—a gesture I would never forget.

Liberation at Last

Liberation finally arrived on May 5, 1945 (the official Liberation Day for the Netherlands), though fighting in our specific area continued for several more days. I have vivid, almost cinematically clear memories of those final battles. The Canadian forces engaged in fierce combat for approximately three days before securing our region. The fighting was particularly intense around various strategic points, as German troops made their last desperate stands.

On April 13, 1945, the Canadian liberation of our region came through what was called "Operation Cannonshot," during which they crossed the IJssel River in their advance toward our town. However, the fighting proved to be exceptionally fierce and the bombardment devastating, largely because the retreating German forces had established their regional headquarters directly in our family home. This strategic positioning made our house a primary military target and forced us to abandon our residence to the occupying army.

The Fatal Bombing

On April 9th, I was next door at my uncle's place, helping him plant potatoes. It should have been routine agricultural work, the kind that continued even during wartime as families struggled to grow enough food to survive. Instead, it became one of the most terrifying and tragic days of my young life.

The British Royal Air Force launched a massive bombing campaign that afternoon, targeting what they believed was still an active German headquarters in our home. However, their intelligence was fatally outdated—the Germans had evacuated just the day before. The Allied pilots had no way of knowing that the strategic target they were ordered to destroy was now simply a family home once again.

I watched in horror as a wave of British bombers appeared on the horizon, their engines creating an ominous thunder that filled the sky. When the bombs began falling, they exploded all around us with earth-shaking force, sending red-hot shrapnel screaming through the air in every direction. My uncle, my cousin, and I threw ourselves to the ground, desperately seeking any protection we could find as metal fragments whistled overhead and chunks of earth rained down upon us. We came terrifyingly close to being killed by the very forces that had come to liberate us.

The Loss of My Beloved Aunt

The most devastating blow came when my beloved aunt became a victim of this tragic friendly fire incident. As the bombing intensified, she heroically tried to shepherd her three daughters—my young cousins—to safety in the cellar. She successfully pushed her daughters ahead of her down the steps, but just as she was about to follow them to safety, shrapnel from an exploding bomb struck her down on the cellar stairs. She died mere feet from the shelter that would have saved her life, sacrificing herself to ensure her children's survival. Her daughters were wounded as well. Shrapnel hit one of them in the leg, and she required hospitalization. The others escaped serious injury.

My uncle's house was severely damaged, and his barn caught fire. The local fire department responded courageously, racing to the scene despite the ongoing air raid. When townspeople saw the fires spreading, they too rushed to help their neighbors. It was then that a second bombardment occurred. The bombs fell among the volunteers and firefighters, killing many of those who had risked their lives to help others. The very act of neighborly assistance became a death sentence for far too many brave souls that day.

That evening, my uncle and his family moved into our cellar, which became even more crowded. The displacement was both physically uncomfortable and emotionally devastating— we had become refugees in our own homeland.

The Agony of Delayed Burial

The days following my aunt's tragic death, our family faced an additional heartbreak that compounded our grief. For several agonizing days, we were unable to give her the dignified burial she deserved. Three separate attempts were made to transport her body to the town cemetery, but each effort had to be abandoned due to the continuing danger from Allied bombardments and ongoing military operations in the area. It would only be after the liberation of our area that we were able to lay her to rest.

The impossibility of conducting this most basic human ritual—laying our beloved family member to rest—added a cruel dimension to our suffering. Death had already taken her from us; now the war was preventing us from honoring her memory with the funeral rites that might have provided some measure of comfort and closure.

Throughout this harrowing period, our extended family sought refuge in the cramped confines of our cellar. The conditions were far from comfortable, but the shared adversity created bonds of mutual support and understanding. Strangers became surrogate family members as we rationed food, shared blankets, and took turns comforting crying children who couldn't understand why their world had been turned upside down.

The Bitter Irony of Liberation

The irony was almost unbearable: after five long years of German occupation, we were finally on the verge of liberation, only to suffer our worst losses at the hands of our would-be liberators, who had no way of knowing that their target was already empty and that innocent civilians were paying the ultimate price for outdated military intelligence.

This reliance on horse-drawn transport revealed just how completely the German war machine had deteriorated by 1945. After years of Allied bombing campaigns targeting fuel depots, refineries, and supply lines, the once-mighty German defense force, the "Wehrmacht," had been reduced to relying on the same transportation methods used by armies centuries earlier. Their trucks, armored vehicles, and motorcycles sat immobilized for lack of fuel, transformed from symbols of mechanized warfare into useless scrap metal.

The sight of German artillery being pulled by farm horses rather than military vehicles served as a powerful visual metaphor for the Third Reich's collapse. These were no longer the confident, well-equipped forces that had rolled across Europe in the early years of the war, but rather a desperate, retreating army making do with whatever resources they could commandeer from the civilian population.

The Final Encirclement

By this stage of the conflict, Holland had become a trap for the remaining German forces. Allied armies had effectively surrounded the country: American and British forces controlled the south and west, while Canadian troops were advancing from the east. The once-proud occupying army now found itself hunted and increasingly isolated, desperately searching for hiding places and escape routes that were rapidly disappearing.

The psychological impact of this encirclement was evident in the German soldiers' behavior. Their earlier arrogance and sense of invincibility had been replaced by nervous energy and barely concealed panic. Every Allied bombing run, every report of advancing enemy troops, every rumor of another German position being overrun added to their mounting anxiety. They were no longer the hunters but the hunted, and they knew that their time was running out.

Terror in Our Own Cellar

During the day on April 13, some German soldiers—about twenty-five of them—tried to take shelter in our cellar, but there was no room for all of us. We were terrified by their guns that seemed trained directly at us. What if they opened fire? They would have eliminated all of us. We were so paralyzed by fear that we couldn't even cry. My father managed to convince them to go to my uncle's house, about half a mile away, which had a much bigger cellar and was empty at the time. They left, to our greatest relief.

Breaking Through the Language Barrier

Late afternoon, on the same day, the Canadian soldiers reached our property, they encountered my father, who faced a significant communication challenge—he couldn't speak a single word of English. However, necessity proved to be the mother of invention. Through an elaborate series of hand gestures, pointing, and improvised sign language, my father managed to convey crucial intelligence to the Canadian forces. He successfully communicated that the German soldiers they were seeking had relocated to my uncle's house and provided clear directions to the location.

That moment represented more than just a language barrier overcome; it symbolized the desperate desire of Dutch civilians to assist their liberators in any way possible, even when formal communication seemed impossible. My father gave the Canadian soldiers a small amount of gin he had saved throughout the entire war as his token of appreciation for the Canadians. We were all excited to see the Canadians.

There was a feed mill in the neighborhood, a farmers' cooperative where grain was ground into animal feed. The Canadians took over and set up a large kitchen where they prepared meals for the soldiers. One day, my mother sent us to ask them for some sugar. For over five years, we hadn't seen sugar. The Canadians gave us several cups of sugar, which was very welcome.

First Encounters with Liberation

Before departing to pursue the Germans, the Canadian soldiers performed a small act of kindness that would remain etched in my memory forever. They tossed several pieces of chewing gum down into our cellar, where we had been taking shelter. This was my very first encounter with chewing gum. This completely foreign concept seemed almost magical to a child who had spent his formative years under the deprivations of wartime rationing.

Even more fascinating was witnessing modern military communication technology in action. One of the Canadian soldiers carried a portable radio—what we would now call a walkie-talkie—equipped with an antenna that extended nearly three feet into the air. We watched in amazement as he spoke into this device, his voice crackling through the static to communicate with other units. The sound of spoken English was entirely new to our ears; after five years of German occupation, hearing this unfamiliar Allied language felt like listening to voices from another world.

As our father provided directions to the Canadian patrol, military operations continued to unfold around us. A reconnaissance aircraft circled overhead, gathering intelligence and coordinating ground movements, while the distinctive rumble of tank engines announced the arrival of Canadian armor rolling through our streets. The mechanical symphony of liberation was finally drowning out the sounds of war.

The Canadian soldiers whom my father had directed to my uncle's property achieved their mission with remarkable efficiency and minimal violence. When they located the German unit, the enemy soldiers chose pragmatism over futile resistance. Rather than risk their lives in a hopeless firefight against superior Allied Forces, they wisely elected to surrender without firing a single shot. These once-intimidating occupiers were quietly taken as prisoners of war, their five-year reign of terror in our region finally at an end.

The contrast was striking: the same German soldiers who had strutted through our home with such arrogance just hours earlier were now defeated prisoners, their maps and communication equipment abandoned, their retreat complete. Liberation had arrived not with the dramatic battle scenes we might have imagined, but with the quiet efficiency of professional soldiers doing their job and enemy forces who recognized that the war was effectively over.

The Final Battle

Our ordeal finally ended on April 13, 1945, when Canadian forces succeeded in completely dislodging the remaining German defenders from our town. The operation was fierce and costly, marking the final chapter of the battle for our region. After days of intense urban warfare, the Canadians had systematically cleared the Germans from their entrenched positions, house by house and street by street.

I remember the exact moment liberation truly arrived: it was in the afternoon of that April 13th when the sounds of gunfire finally ceased, and Canadian soldiers appeared in our street, no longer as pursuing forces but as victorious liberators securing a conquered town.

The victory, however, came at a terrible price. During this final assault, the Canadian forces lost their commanding officer, Lieutenant Colonel McKenzie, who was killed in action while leading his troops in the liberation of our town. His death represented the ultimate irony of war—he had traveled thousands of miles from his homeland to free strangers in a foreign country, only to give his life just as victory was within reach. Today, there is a commemorative plaque in the town of Wilp, about a mile and a half from my town, serving as a permanent reminder of the sacrifice made by this Canadian officer and other Canadian soldiers who died so that we might live in freedom.

CHAPTER 3

A Nation in Mourning

* * *

My family's suffering during the war was not unique—virtually every household in Holland endured devastating losses and hardships that would scar them for generations. As the conflict dragged on and intensified, the economic infrastructure of daily life completely collapsed. Even families fortunate enough to have saved money discovered that currency had become meaningless when there was simply nothing left to purchase. Store shelves stood empty, markets closed, and the necessities of life became increasingly scarce or entirely unavailable.

The human cost was even more staggering than the material deprivation. There was scarcely a family in our town, or indeed throughout the Netherlands, that had not been forced to mourn the death of at least one beloved family member. The war had touched every household with its cold hand, leaving behind a trail of grief that would persist long after the guns fell silent.

Following the devastating bombing that claimed my aunt's life, my uncle faced the overwhelming challenge of raising his children as a single father while simultaneously grieving the loss of his wife. In response to his desperate situation, he moved his entire family into our already crowded home, nearly doubling the household's size overnight.

The Burden of Feeding Many

This arrangement placed enormous additional burdens on my mother, who suddenly found herself responsible for preparing meals for what seemed like an army of hungry mouths. The logistics alone were daunting—portioning out limited ingredients, stretching them, and ensuring everyone received adequate nutrition despite severe wartime shortages. Fortunately, one of my uncle's older daughters, mature beyond her years given the circumstances, stepped forward to assist my mother with household management, cooking, and supervising the younger children.

The temporary living arrangement continued for several months, lasting until the Canadian forces had established firm control over our region and everyday civilian life began to resume. Only when stability returned, and reconstruction efforts began in earnest, did my uncle feel confident enough to move his family back to their own home, which had been damaged but not destroyed in the bombing.

Watching my cousins navigate daily life without their mother was heartbreaking. The absence of her gentle guidance, loving comfort, and maternal wisdom left a void that no amount of support from extended family could fill. Their loss served as a constant reminder of the war's capacity to shatter not just buildings and infrastructure, but the very fabric of family life itself.

As the oldest child in a family of seven, I inherited responsibilities that would have been considered excessive for someone my age under normal circumstances. However, wartime had a way of forcing children to mature rapidly, and survival often depended on every family member—regardless of age—contributing to the household's functioning.

One of my primary daily responsibilities involved preparing the potatoes that had become our dietary staple throughout the war years. These hardy tubers formed the foundation of virtually every meal we consumed, day after day, month after month. Each evening before retiring to bed, I would methodically peel an entire bucket full of potatoes by the dim light of our kerosene lamps, preparing them for the following day's meals. It was monotonous work, but absolutely essential for our family's survival.

The war had stripped away many of the basic conveniences that we had previously taken for granted. Electricity was either unavailable or severely rationed, forcing us to rely on kerosene lamps for illumination during the long, dark evenings. Maintaining these lamps became another of my regular duties—each night, I would carefully fill them with precious kerosene, trim the wicks to ensure clean burning, and keep them lit to provide adequate light for the household's evening activities.

These tasks might seem simple in retrospect, but they required constant attention and carried real consequences if neglected. A lamp that ran out of fuel could plunge the family into darkness, while improperly maintained wicks could produce dangerous smoke and soot.

Additionally, every Saturday morning, I was entrusted with another important family responsibility that made me feel both grown-up and essential: traveling to the town drugstore to purchase vital supplies for our bustling household. These weekly expeditions involved carefully gathering items from a mental checklist—medicines for various ailments, cotton bandages for scraped knees and everyday injuries, bottles of sharp-smelling rubbing alcohol, and an array of other necessities that my mother required to maintain our family's health and well-being.

For a young boy navigating the adult world of merchants and transactions, being given this level of responsibility represented both a profound mark of parental trust and a practical necessity in a household where my mother was constantly occupied caring for seven energetic children. I took immense pride in counting out coins, checking items off lists, and returning home with everything exactly as requested.

A Mother's Overwhelming Burden

My mother faced challenges that would have tested the limits of even the most capable parent. She had given birth to seven children in rapid succession during some of the most difficult years in Dutch history, and now found herself responsible for their physical, emotional, and spiritual well-being while also managing an expanded household that included my uncle's family.

My younger brothers and sisters, still too small to handle the heavier household chores or contribute meaningful assistance with outdoor farm work, naturally required more care than they could provide in return. This reality meant that much of the responsibility for supporting my mother's Herculean efforts fell to me as the eldest child.

The expectations placed upon me were substantial, but I understood intuitively that our family's survival depended on everyone fulfilling their role to the best of their ability. In a world where adult authority figures were struggling to maintain basic order and security, children like me were forced to step up and assume responsibilities that would have been unthinkable in peacetime. It was not a childhood in any conventional sense, but rather a premature initiation into the harsh realities of adult life.

The Art of Wartime Gardening

My father exemplified the work ethic and resourcefulness that enabled so many Dutch families to survive wartime hardships. His daily routine began before dawn—he would rise promptly at 5 a.m., consume a simple breakfast, and immediately head outside to tend our family garden. This small plot of land, situated just beside our house, represented far more than a hobby or pastime; it was our lifeline to adequate nutrition during the lean war years.

Despite the garden's modest dimensions, my father possessed an almost magical ability to coax extraordinary yields from this limited space. His deep understanding of soil conditions, crop rotation, plant spacing, and seasonal timing allowed him to maximize every square meter of available growing area. What should have been a typical small backyard garden somehow produced harvests that consistently amazed our entire family and even impressed our neighbors.

My father's agricultural expertise became increasingly crucial as traditional food distribution systems collapsed under the pressures of occupation and warfare. While neighboring families struggled with severe shortages and rationed meals, our household enjoyed a relative abundance of fresh potatoes, carrots, beans, and leafy vegetables—all thanks entirely to his exceptional skill and unwavering dedication.

He seemed to possess an almost mystical understanding of the land, an intuitive knowledge of exactly when to plant each variety, when to harvest at peak nutrition, and how to store crops in makeshift root cellars to ensure a continuous food supply throughout the harsh, unpredictable seasons of wartime.

His remarkable success wasn't merely a matter of luck or favorable weather—it reflected decades of accumulated farming wisdom, careful observation of subtle natural patterns, and an almost scientific approach to maximizing productivity from the most limited resources. He could coax abundance from poor soil, stretch seeds beyond their expected yield, and somehow make barren patches bloom with life.

During an era when every calorie was precious and fresh vegetables were often unavailable at any price in the devastated markets, his gardening prowess represented nothing less than the difference between adequate nutrition and the gnawing hunger that haunted so many families around us.

Seeds of a Lifelong Passion

Working alongside my father in that small but remarkably productive garden, planted the seeds of what would become a lifelong love affair with the soil. As I helped him prepare beds with makeshift tools, carefully plant precious seeds saved from previous harvests, tend growing plants with improvised fertilizers, and harvest the literal fruits of our shared labor, I absorbed not only practical agricultural techniques but also a profound appreciation for the deep satisfaction that comes from nurturing life from the earth.

Those early morning hours spent working side by side in the garden—learning to distinguish between valuable seedlings and invasive weeds, understanding the critical importance of proper watering schedules and creative fertilization methods, and experiencing the pure excitement of watching tiny, seemingly lifeless seeds transform into substantial food crops—created indelible memories that would influence my interests, values, and hobbies for decades to come.

The gardening passion that I maintain to this day, now in my own backyard and greenhouse, can be traced directly back to those formative experiences during those difficult war years. What began as a family's desperate survival strategy became a source of immense family pride, a masterclass in resourcefulness, and a profound education in the fundamental, sacred relationship between human effort and the natural world.

What started as a child's simple obligation to help feed his family gradually evolved into something far more meaningful—a lifelong appreciation for both the art and science of growing things, a deep connection to the earth that continues to bring me joy, peace, and satisfaction many decades later. In every seed I plant today, I honor my father's legacy and remember the garden that sustained us when the world seemed to be falling apart.

Bicycles: The Lifeline of a Nation

During the peaceful years before the war, bicycles were the undisputed primary mode of transportation throughout Holland, forming the backbone of daily mobility for families, workers, students, and virtually everyone in between. The Netherlands' famously flat terrain and extensive, well-maintained network of dedicated bike paths made cycling both supremely practical and remarkably efficient for covering the substantial distances between towns, farms, schools, and neighborhoods.

Children learned to ride before they could walk properly. Workers pedaled to factories in orderly streams each morning. Families loaded bikes with groceries, children, and parcels. The gentle whir of bicycle chains and the soft ring of handlebar bells created the soundtrack of Dutch daily life.

When War Stole Our Wheels

However, the war years brought devastating shortages that affected even this most fundamental form of transportation, disrupting a way of life that had endured for generations. Bicycles became virtually impossible to obtain through any legitimate means, as did the simplest replacement parts—tires, inner tubes, chains, bearings, brake cables, and even basic repair tools.

Existing bikes were systematically commandeered by German occupation forces for their own transportation needs, requisitioned for the broader war effort, or simply worn out beyond any hope of repair, with absolutely no possibility of restoration or replacement. Families watched helplessly as their primary means of independence and mobility was stripped away, leaving them stranded and dependent.

The absence of reliable transportation transformed even simple errands like my weekly drugstore trips into increasingly challenging expeditions that required careful planning, alternative routes, and often the kindness of neighbors willing to share rides or carry extra supplies.

A Tenth Birthday to Remember

My first bicycle finally materialized when I turned ten years old, making it not just a birthday gift but a small miracle orchestrated by my father's persistence and resourcefulness. Given the severe wartime shortages that had gripped our country for years, simply finding even a used bicycle represented both a significant accomplishment and a substantial financial investment for our family, whose budget was already stretched thin by the demands of feeding and clothing seven children.

New bicycles were simply nonexistent in any marketplace, relegated to the realm of fantasy and peacetime memories. A secondhand, well-worn model wasn't just the economical choice—it was literally the only option available to families like ours who couldn't access black-market goods or military connections.

When the much-anticipated bicycle was finally delivered to our front door, my excitement reached an almost unbearable fever pitch. I had dreamed of this moment for months, imagining the freedom and adventure that awaited me on two wheels. The bike looked genuinely impressive at first glance—someone had invested considerable effort in making it presentable, coating it with a fresh layer of sleek black paint that gleamed in the afternoon sunlight, giving it an almost factory-new appearance.

However, my father's experienced and practical eye, honed by years of mechanical work and wartime resourcefulness, immediately detected serious problems that the cosmetic improvements had been carefully designed to conceal from less knowledgeable buyers.

Upon his methodical closer inspection—checking joints, testing moving parts, examining the frame for stress fractures— he discovered that the bicycle's essential bearings were not just worn but severely deteriorated, rendering them unsafe for operation. In his measured professional judgment, the structural integrity of the entire bike was so fundamentally compromised that it could literally disintegrate while being ridden, potentially sending his young son tumbling onto hard pavement or into traffic.

Despite the appealing fresh paint job that made it visually attractive to a child's eager eyes, the bicycle was mechanically unsound, structurally unsafe, and entirely unsuitable for regular use by anyone, let alone his ten-year-old boy, who would depend on it for daily transportation and weekend adventures.

The Weight of a Father's Decision

My father's decision to reject the bicycle was both firm and absolutely non-negotiable. In his mind, safety took complete and unwavering precedence over my eager anticipation and birthday excitement, even though this meant crushing the spirits of his ten-year-old son on what should have been one of the happiest days of his young life.

The disappointment I felt was profound and overwhelming—a deep, aching sadness that settled in my chest and refused to lift. After years of watching other children effortlessly glide past our house on their bicycles, after countless dreams of the freedom and independence that cycling would provide, after imagining myself joining the ranks of mobile children who could explore beyond walking distance, I was forced to wait even longer for this fundamental milestone of childhood.

I struggled to understand how something that looked so promising, so shiny and new, could be deemed unworthy. The gap between my child's perception and my father's adult wisdom felt insurmountable, leaving me caught between disappointment and a grudging respect for his unwavering commitment to my safety.

Finally, a Reliable Companion

The extended wait proved entirely worthwhile when, on my eagerly anticipated eleventh birthday, my father presented me with a significantly better bicycle—one that not only met but exceeded his exacting standards for both safety and long-term reliability. This second bicycle, though perhaps less flashy than its predecessor, possessed the solid construction and dependable mechanics that would serve me faithfully for years to come.

This carefully chosen bicycle became far more than mere transportation; it evolved into a source of immense pride and pure joy, representing not just a mode of getting from place to place but a powerful symbol of my growing independence, increasing responsibility, and my father's trust in my developing maturity.

I rode that bicycle with tremendous satisfaction and deep gratitude, knowing that my father's meticulous judgment and patient search had ensured I possessed a truly reliable companion for all the adventures, errands, and explorations that lay ahead. The extra year of enforced waiting had only intensified my appreciation for this precious gift, teaching me that good things truly do come to those who wait.

With the wisdom that comes only through time and experience, I gradually came to understand that my father's initial rejection of the unsafe bicycle had been neither arbitrary criticism nor needless perfectionism, but rather a profound act of love, protection, and parental responsibility. He had chosen to endure his son's tears and disappointment rather than risk his physical safety—a decision that required both courage and conviction. That seemingly harsh birthday disappointment became one of my earliest lessons in the difference between what we want and what we truly need, between surface appearances and underlying quality, and between immediate gratification and patient wisdom that considers long-term consequences over momentary desires.

Grandmother's Special Day

One of my most treasured errands occurred with clockwork precision every November 3rd—my beloved grandmother's birthday. My mother, invariably overwhelmed by the relentless demands of managing our large, boisterous family, would entrust me with the most special task of all: delivering birthday flowers to her mother, who lived an hour's bicycle ride away.

My grandmother harbored a particular fondness for chrysanthemums, those resilient autumn flowers that burst into magnificent blooms during her November birthday month. Their rich yellows, deep oranges, and burgundy petals seemed to capture the very essence of the season, and she would beam with delight whenever these hardy flowers appeared at her doorstep.

I have crystal-clear memories of carefully cradling those precious chrysanthemums during what must have been one of my earliest solo bicycle rides to my grandmother's house. Wobbling slightly as I navigated the familiar streets, the responsibility of delivering this birthday tribute felt tremendously important—almost sacred. I took extraordinary pride in ensuring that every petal arrived in perfect condition and that not a single flower head was damaged during my careful journey.

38

CHAPTER 4

Disrupted Education and Lost Opportunities

* * *

The war years severely disrupted the Dutch educational system, leaving many children with significant gaps in their formal schooling. When normal classes finally resumed, our school year was scheduled to begin on April 1st. However, due to an inflexible age-requirement policy, I was informed that, because my birthday fell on April 8th—just one week after the start of the academic year—I would not be permitted to enroll until the following year.

This arbitrary cutoff date meant that I lost an entire year of education through no fault of my own. The timing seemed particularly cruel: after already missing substantial schooling during the occupation years, I was forced to wait another full year simply because I had been born eight days too late in the calendar. This setback would have lasting consequences for my educational trajectory and contribute to my eventual decision to leave school earlier than I otherwise might have.

Early Introduction to Smoking

It was during this period of limited schooling and increased free time that I was first introduced to cigarette smoking at the remarkably young age of thirteen. In the context of 1940s Holland, this early initiation into smoking was not considered particularly unusual or shocking. Dutch society at the time held much more permissive attitudes toward youth smoking than would be acceptable today.

While smoking was strictly prohibited within school buildings and classrooms, once we stepped outside the school grounds, children and teenagers were free to smoke openly without significant adult intervention or social disapproval. However, cigarettes, like many other items, were not readily available.

As we grew older and gained access to bicycles, smoking became intertwined with our sense of independence and adventure. My friends and I would embark on lengthy bicycle journeys, covering considerable distances across the Dutch countryside, with the primary purpose of meeting up with other young smokers to share cigarettes and enjoy what we perceived as sophisticated adult behavior.

These cycling expeditions represented more than just opportunities to smoke; they symbolized our growing autonomy and our desire to explore the world beyond our immediate neighborhoods. The combination of the physical freedom our bicycles provided and the perceived sophistication of smoking created a powerful sense of rebellion and maturity that was intoxicating for teenagers emerging from the restrictions and uncertainties of wartime.

One particular incident from my smoking days remains vividly etched in my memory, both for its potential danger and its absurd comedy. I had ridden my bicycle into the school courtyard while carelessly smoking a cigarette, completely forgetting about the strict prohibition against tobacco use on school property.

When I suddenly realized my mistake and the very real possibility of being caught by a teacher or administrator, panic set in immediately. In my haste to conceal the evidence, I attempted to extinguish the cigarette quickly, but my nervous fumbling failed to put it out completely. Desperate to hide the still-glowing cigarette from potential discovery, I shoved it hastily into my trouser pocket and hurried into the school building.

The consequences of this ill-conceived plan became apparent during class, when I began to feel what seemed like a sharp, persistent sting on my leg. When I discreetly reached into my pocket to investigate, I discovered to my horror that the cigarette butt was still smoldering. It had burned a substantial hole through both my pocket handkerchief and a portion of my trousers, creating unmistakable evidence of my smoking transgression.

Faced with the prospect of explaining this damage to my mother—who would undoubtedly deduce the true cause of the mysterious burn holes—I resorted to creative damage control. I carefully cut away the burned sections of my trousers in a pattern that might plausibly be attributed to an accidental tear or snag rather than a smoking-related incident. While my friends and I later found great humor in this close call, the incident served as an early lesson in both the practical dangers of careless smoking and the complications that arise when attempting to conceal risky behavior from parents.

The Path to Quitting

Fortunately, I did not remain a smoker for an extended period. As scientific understanding of smoking's health risks became more widely known and accepted, I recognized the wisdom of abandoning this dangerous habit. However, breaking free from nicotine addiction proved more challenging than simply acknowledging its harmful effects. I was twenty-six years old when I finally succeeded in quitting smoking permanently. By that time, I had already been living in the United States for seven years, having emigrated from Holland at the age of nineteen. The decision to quit smoking represented part of a broader pattern of personal growth and adaptation that characterized my early years in America, as I worked to establish healthier habits and build a new life in my adopted country.

I left school on my 15th birthday, choosing instead to work and earn an income to supplement what my father was bringing home, which was no longer sufficient. With so many mouths to feed, I felt it necessary to contribute financially as well.

I was keen to work in a nursery or on a farm, and I secured a position on a farm that provided room and board. This arrangement meant one fewer mouth to feed at home, which brought considerable relief to my mother. Each month, I would take my entire wages to her, modest though they were. She would keep a portion and return the remainder to me. I returned home every other weekend, and I always felt a deep satisfaction watching my mother receive what I brought with such evident joy. There was something profoundly fulfilling about bringing happiness to my mother and witnessing the tangible relief that my earnings provided.

Weekend Journeys Home

Every other weekend, I would make the long journey home—a three-hour bicycle ride that became both a physical challenge and a cherished ritual. The routine was always the same: I'd finish work at 3 p.m. on Saturday, quickly gather my belongings, and set off by 5 p.m. for the familiar road that led home. The miles stretched ahead of me as I pedaled through the countryside, my legs growing heavy with fatigue, but my heart lightening with each mile that brought me closer to family.

By 8 p.m., I would finally arrive, exhausted but grateful, wheeling my bicycle up to the house where warm lights promised rest and reunion. The weariness in my bones seemed a small price to pay for these precious hours with my loved ones.

Sunday afternoons brought the inevitable return journey. At 4 p.m., I would reluctantly push off again, retracing the same route that would deliver me back to work by 7 p.m. But these return trips held a special magic—my father would often join me for the first several miles, our bicycles moving in a comfortable rhythm as we shared what would become our most meaningful conversations.

During these precious miles together, we would talk about everything and nothing: my work, his hopes for me, and dreams for the future. The steady cadence of our pedaling seemed to unlock something between us, creating a sacred space for the kind of father-son conversations that might never have happened within the confines of home. There was one particularly memorable evening when he rode much farther than usual, so caught up in our discussion that he had to make the long journey back home alone in the gathering dusk.

The Apple Harvest

One autumn day brought an unexpected treasure: I was permitted to take home a burlap sack full of fresh apples—a luxury we rarely enjoyed at home. I can still remember the weight of that sack, growing heavier with each mile, the apples shifting and settling with every bump in the road. My arms ached, my back strained, and more than once I was tempted to abandon my burden by the roadside, telling myself that no one would know.

But then I would think of how I collected those apples earlier that morning. More importantly, I would picture my family's faces when I arrived—the delight in my mother's eyes, the eager hands reaching for the rare treat, the way we would all gather around as she planned how to make the most of this unexpected bounty. That vision gave me the strength to continue, adjusting the sack on my shoulders and pushing forward, one pedal stroke at a time. The apples were received with exactly the joy and gratitude I had imagined, making every aching mile worthwhile.

A Summer Tradition is Born

When I was home during the warm summer weekends, I would take my two younger sisters, eight-year-old Riekie and six-year-old Betsy, on special expeditions to pick wild blackberries. These adventures became some of our most treasured times together. I would lead them to the best spots I had discovered—hidden patches where the berries grew fat and sweet, away from the well-traveled paths where others might have already harvested the choicest fruit.

My sisters would chatter excitedly as we filled our containers, their small fingers quickly learning to distinguish the perfectly ripe berries from those that needed a few more days of sun. They would inevitably eat as many as they collected, returning home with purple-stained mouths and full hearts, carrying enough berries for our mother to transform into precious jars of jam that would brighten our winter meals.

What strikes me most profoundly now is that this simple tradition I began with them has endured across the decades. Today, both sisters are in their eighties—Riekie in California, Betsy back in Holland—yet they both continue to venture out each summer to pick berries and make jam, just as we did all those years ago. The knowledge and joy I shared with them during those childhood expeditions planted seeds that have borne fruit for a lifetime. In teaching them to find nature's bounty and transform it into something precious for the family table, I gave them a gift that has enriched not only their own lives but also the lives of their children and grandchildren. Sometimes the smallest acts of guidance we offer to those we love create the most enduring legacies.

The farm work also gave me the chance to save a little money—something I had never been able to do before. With those modest earnings, I was finally able to purchase items I had long admired but could never afford. My first indulgence was a fountain pen, a simple object yet one that carried enormous meaning for me. I had always yearned to own one, to feel its weight in my hand, to see my handwriting transformed by its smooth, elegant ink. Later, after many more weeks of careful saving, I treated myself to a watch. To this day, I can still recall the thrill of fastening it around my wrist, not because of its monetary value, but because it was mine—bought with my own hard-earned money. There was a tremendous satisfaction in knowing that I no longer had to ask anyone for such things. These purchases were tangible proof of my independence, earned through honest labor and genuine effort.

A Quiet Passion for Horticulture

I remained on that first farm for two years before moving on to a new opportunity. When I finally announced my decision to leave, the family who employed me seemed genuinely sad. They had grown accustomed to my presence and, having witnessed my diligence, had hoped I would stay on indefinitely. "You are like family to us," they told me, urging me to reconsider. Their warmth and sincerity made it difficult to part ways, but my mind was already set on pursuing something closer to my heart.

For as long as I could remember, I had nurtured a quiet passion for horticulture. Yet the farm where I had been working grew only the most basic crops—vegetables and many kinds of fruits and berries. Flowers, which fascinated me, were nowhere to be found. The prospect of joining another farm, one that specialized in cultivating and selling flowers, was irresistible. What made this new location even more enticing was that I could take a two-year diploma-level course in horticulture. The program promised not only hands-on experience but also formal training in greenhouse construction and the commercial cultivation of flowers. The opportunity was in the western part of Holland, nearly 100 miles from my hometown—a considerable distance for someone of my means, but I felt it was the right path for me. I was 17 years old at the time.

The move meant a new rhythm to life. Gone were the weekends when I could regularly return home. Now, visits were reduced to once every six weeks, a change made more challenging by the expense of travel. Train tickets were far beyond my budget, so I relied on hitchhiking instead. Occasionally, I was fortunate enough to catch rides on delivery trucks heading in the direction of my hometown, though these journeys were never predictable. Many times I found myself arriving long after midnight, sometimes not until two in the morning.

Not wishing to disturb my family at such an ungodly hour, I would quietly slip into the house through an upstairs window that was never fully secured. My mother would always discover me the following morning, and her reaction became a familiar mixture of joy and concern. She was delighted to see me, yet at the same time could not help but scold me gently for the dangers of hitchhiking at night. "It is not safe for someone your age," she would say, her worry etched clearly in her voice. That blend of maternal love and anxiety became a small ritual during those brief visits home, and I cherished it all the same.

By the time I eventually left home for good, life in our village had begun to change in small but significant ways. In 1953, electricity finally reached our houses. The arrival of this new convenience was almost magical to us. We really also needed a radio, but could not afford one. My younger brother and I, unwilling to be left behind in this modern age, began searching through rubbish dumps for discarded radios. We salvaged what parts we could—especially the tubes—and spent hours tinkering with them. Sometimes we managed to buy old replacements at the flea market, exchanging them until we found one that worked. The excitement we felt when even the faintest sound emerged from the battered speakers was indescribable. To us, it was as though we had captured a voice from the air itself, and in those moments, the world felt just a little bigger, a little closer.

My Mother and Me in 1938

Mulder Brothers in 1942. Left to right:
Teun, Jan and Henry

Mulder Brothers in 1956:
Left to right: Henry, Teun
and Jan

Grandma Mulder

My Maternal
Granparents
(Siemelink)

My Parents: Henricus
(Hein); my father and
Henrica (Riek), my mother.
Picture taken on their
wedding day in 1936

Me at 15 in 1954

Me at 19 in 1957

Top: Mulder Children in 1953; bottom: Mulder Children in 1997. The two pictures above were taken on the same spot and in the same order, 44 years apart.

A picture of our house that I took using my new camera in 1957.

Saint Martinus Catholic School of our city Twello

Saint Martinus
Catholic Church of
our city Twello

Twello, my town's
grain grinding
windmill

CHAPTER 5

America, Here We Come!

* * *

When I was working in a nursery in western Holland that cultivated only vegetables in greenhouses, I met someone who would become a dear friend, Peter van Os. We worked together for several years before making the momentous decision to emigrate to California. This was an era when countless people from Holland sought new opportunities abroad, departing for destinations such as Australia, Canada, and New Zealand. While sometimes entire families would uproot themselves, in our case, it was simply the two of us embarking on this adventure.

Initially, Peter and I discussed the prospect of emigrating abroad in quite casual terms, treating it more as a distant dream than a concrete plan. However, in June 1956, I heard a radio announcement stating that it was possible to find an American sponsor who could facilitate one's settlement in the United States. Motivated by this news, I cycled to the nearest post office,

15 minutes away, to telephone the immigration bureau at the US Embassy in Rotterdam for further details. That telephone call marked a significant milestone—it was the very first call I had ever made in my life. Through this inquiry, I was put in contact with a Catholic immigration organization, which subsequently invited me to visit their office.

The post-war period of the 1950s witnessed an unprecedented wave of Dutch emigration, driven by a complex web of economic, social, and psychological factors. The Netherlands, despite its remarkable recovery from wartime devastation, faced significant challenges, including overpopulation, limited agricultural land, and economic uncertainty that made emigration an attractive prospect for many young people. The Dutch government actively encouraged this exodus through various programs and policies, viewing it as a means to alleviate population pressure while providing opportunities for its citizens to prosper abroad.

For young men like Peter and me, emigration represented more than mere economic opportunity—it embodied the quintessential post-war spirit of reinvention and boundless possibility. The decision to leave behind familiar landscapes, family ties, and cultural moorings required considerable courage, particularly for individuals from rural backgrounds who had rarely ventured far from their birthplaces. Yet the allure of the American dream, with its promise of social mobility and vast agricultural frontiers, proved irresistible. Our friendship became the foundation upon which we built our shared vision of a new life, transforming casual workplace conversations into a concrete plan that would forever alter the trajectory of our lives. The very act of making that first telephone call represented a symbolic crossing of the threshold from dreaming to doing, marking the beginning of a journey that would test our resilience, determination, and the strength of our bond.

My friend and I were summoned for an interview at the US Embassy in Rotterdam. The questions centered primarily on our political affiliations and wartime experiences. They needed to ascertain whether we had any connections to the Nazis or communists. What had we done during the war? Had we suffered in any way during the conflict? These were standard but crucial inquiries in the Cold War climate of the 1950s. The post-war emigration interviews conducted by American embassies across Europe reflected the intense geopolitical anxieties of the emerging Cold War era. These screening processes were designed not merely to assess applicants' suitability for immigration, but to serve as crucial filters against potential security threats during a period of heightened international tension. The specific focus on Nazi and communist affiliations stemmed from America's dual concerns: preventing former Nazi collaborators from entering the country, while simultaneously guarding against communist infiltration.

For young Dutch applicants like ourselves, these questions carried particular weight, given the Netherlands' complex wartime experience under German occupation, in which the population had been forced into various forms of accommodation, resistance, or collaboration. We were granted three-month visas and would board a ship bound for New York Harbor.

Crossing the Atlantic

A month before our scheduled departure, I received a call-up notice to join the Dutch army for mandatory national service. I immediately went to the military authorities to request a dispensation, explaining that I had already received a visa and was about to emigrate to the United States. Fortunately, my request was granted, allowing me to proceed with our emigration plans.

On our departure date, February 16, 1957, my family accompanied me on the lengthy journey to Rotterdam, over 100 miles from our hometown. My friend Peter Van Os was more fortunate in this regard, as he lived considerably closer to the port—only about 30 miles away. When we arrived at the harbor, he and his family were already waiting. The farewell proved deeply emotional, as this marked the first time any of us had ever left Holland's shores. It was genuinely heartbreaking to bid goodbye to our families, particularly knowing that we had no certainty of ever returning home again.

After a tearful farewell from my parents and family members, we boarded the "Zuiderkruis" at about 1:00 p.m. We were shown to our cabin, number 330, which we shared with four other young men. Pete and I occupied one of the double bunks, with Pete taking the top one. At 1:30 p.m., we were served lunch, which was very good. At 3:30 p.m., the gangplank was lifted, and after three blasts of the steam whistle, we set sail. We waved goodbye until my family was out of sight, then sailed through the Nieuwe Waterweg toward Hoek van Holland. Peter's brothers awaited us in Maassluis, by the Poorsters Haven. We waved goodbye to them with our red handkerchiefs, as we had promised.

It was almost 6:00 p.m. when we arrived at Hoek van Holland and entered the North Sea. After dinner, we explored the ship to familiarize ourselves with our surroundings. Around 10:00 p.m., we went to bed, but falling asleep was difficult after such an emotional day and in a strange bed.

During the night, the clock was set back one hour, so it was nearly daylight by 6:00 a.m. Sunday morning began with Mass at 7:30. It was a beautiful, sunny morning with calm seas. After breakfast around 9:00 a.m., we went up to the deck to enjoy the sunshine. Pete started to feel a bit seasick, but after throwing up, he felt somewhat better.

Throughout the day, we visited the onboard chaplain, who gave us a National Catholic Welfare Conference (NCWC) pin so people in New York would recognize us and assist us with the rest of our journey. In New York, we would learn our final destination. For the rest of the day, it was a quiet Sunday. In the evening, I watched a movie while Peter went to bed early. After the movie, we set the clock back another hour, so I wasn't too late getting to bed. Those were long days—each day seemed to stretch an hour longer.

The next day, Monday morning, I still felt okay after a good night's rest. I attended Mass again at 6:30, but Pete, who was getting quite seasick, spent almost the entire day in bed. That evening, the sea started to get rougher, and I found it difficult to keep food down. It was supposed to be a dance night, but it was canceled as most of the women and girls were starting to feel ill. With no activities planned, I went to bed early.

After a good night's sleep, I felt very fit the next morning, which was Tuesday. There was much to do on the ship: a library, a chess competition, card games, and recorded music all day long. Each morning, we attended the 6:30 morning Mass and a general evening prayer at 8 pm. The food was excellent, with bread for breakfast and warm meals for lunch and dinner, accompanied by fruit or ice cream for dessert. In the mornings, coffee, hot chocolate, and milk were available, and tea was served in the afternoon.

On Tuesday evening, there was dancing, and everyone had a wonderful time. Even though I had danced on many different floors before, I had never danced on a moving floor. It was not easy, as you slid from one end to the other with the ship's movement. While it may not have been the best dancing, it was entertaining and helped me forget I was on a ship, allowing me to manage my seasickness better.

Peter was still feeling awful. During the night from Tuesday to Wednesday, the clock was set back 42 minutes. I slept well that night. On Wednesday morning, before breakfast, I went to see the doctor for medication for terrible sores in my mouth, which were already painful and making me uncomfortable. He provided me with pills, mouthwash, and an injection, asking me to return the next morning for another injection. The weather was pleasant that day, and we were able to sit on deck in the sunshine. All we could see was water and more water. However, the weather turned bad in the evening. The wind picked up, and the sea became rough; we could barely stand up. It was essential to watch what we ate, as it was difficult to keep it down. That evening, we played Bingo, which I had never played before. It was fun, especially since I won four guilders. That night, the clock was set back another 44 minutes.

On Thursday morning, I went to see the doctor early for my injection. The doctor's office was very busy because many passengers were sick. It was a very rough day, and we cruised at half power. If you managed to get to the rear of the ship, you would be moving as much as 30 feet up and down. I had been told when I was younger that a ship at sea during a severe storm looked like half-a-nut shell. Out of curiosity, I crawled on deck on my hands and knees just to see for myself. It was true; the ship looked very tiny between the towering waves. It was scary, but I did not feel sick. Peter stayed in bed that whole day.

I took pictures, but the photographer could not develop them because the sea was too rough. That evening, there was no music; the needle couldn't stay on the record, so we went to bed early. We still had 1,758 miles to reach our destination. During the night, we traveled only 4 miles per hour, which meant a delay of several days.

The next morning, Friday, February 22nd, the sea was a little calmer, but not by much. That day, I washed some clothes, especially handkerchiefs, as I had a terrible cold. In the evening, the ship stopped due to an engine room problem. A movie scheduled for that evening was canceled, but was shown later as the sea calmed. That night, the clock was set back another 21 minutes.

The following day, Saturday, the weather improved, and we were sailing faster. By then, we had already been on board for a week and still had 1,285 miles to go. Peter stayed in bed; each time he tried to get up, he would throw up. In the evening, I brought him something from the dining room; usually, all he wanted was an orange. For lunch, food was brought to the cabins for those who were sick. There were many Catholics on board, and almost all of them attended Mass.

Each morning, we received a newsletter called the "Ocean Post," which contained news that had come in overnight from Radio Scheveningen. That Sunday evening, we were served a delicious farewell dinner: fried chicken and baked ice cream. Yes, the food on board was delicious, but unfortunately, many of us lacked the appetite to enjoy it. That evening was pleasant, with a live show. The clock was set back another 35 minutes. We had a good night's rest, and the following day, Monday, we were informed that we might arrive on Tuesday and possibly disembark on Wednesday. The ocean was much calmer, and we watched a nice movie about Louis Armstrong that evening.

On Tuesday morning, we set the clocks back 55 minutes, having traveled quickly over the past 24 hours, covering 400 miles. The first thing that morning, I saw the doctor for one last injection. My mouth hadn't worsened, but it hadn't improved much either. The weather was pleasant, allowing us to sit on deck without jackets or sweaters. The ocean was as smooth as a mirror.

That evening was our last chance to dance, and we also needed to spend our onboard money. As a result, there was quite a bit of drinking, and everyone had a great time. On Wednesday morning, we attended Mass at 5:15 a.m. We were informed that it was held early because the hall needed to be prepared by 8 o'clock for the American immigration authorities, who would be boarding the ship.

However, at 8:00 a.m., the ship had to drop anchor due to dense fog. We couldn't get a pilot aboard, so we had to wait until noon for the fog to lift before we could continue. Around 4:00 p.m., we saw the Statue of Liberty and the country that awaited us. What a profoundly emotional moment that was for all of us! We had, at long last, reached the United States of America—the Land of the Free! The sight of Lady Liberty, her torch held high in welcome, seemed to validate every hardship we had endured on our journey and to symbolize the promise of the new life that awaited us. Through the fog, the tall buildings of Manhattan came into view. What a sight, it was!

CHAPTER 6

Give Me Your Tired Ones!

***

There was a strike at the New York harbor, and no tugboats were available, so our ship had to enter the harbor under its own power, which took a long time. It was almost 7:00 p.m. when we finally moored on February 28, 1957. It was already too late to disembark, so we had to spend that night aboard. That evening on deck was beautiful. Everywhere you looked, there was a sea of lights. Our immigration organization later informed us that Gustine, California, would be our final destination. We were thrilled to finally learn where we would end up; we were surprised to hear that California was our destination. That meant a long train ride across a significant portion of the United States.

Once we were released, we were taken by bus to a railroad station in New Jersey. At 5 p.m., we boarded the Baltimore and Ohio train, which took us to Chicago, arriving at 3:30 p.m.

The journey offered little scenery, just a winter landscape with snow covering everything. Closer to Chicago, we saw large steel plants, highlighting the city's industrial nature. We spent the afternoon in Chicago waiting to board the next train at 6:30 p.m. It was a large Union Pacific train that would cross the prairies and take us to San Francisco.

Our train finally departed for California, a journey that would span four days across the United States. We were traveling in second-class accommodations, equipped with nothing more than hard wooden benches that served the dual purpose of seats during the day and makeshift beds at night. We used our heavy overcoats as blankets to ward off the chill and fashioned pillows from our thick woolen sweaters. However, being merely 19 years old at the time, we possessed the resilience and adaptability of youth, enabling us to endure the physical discomforts of such arduous travel without significant difficulty. Undoubtedly though, our principal challenge was that we scarcely knew any English whatsoever.

February's grip still held much of the nation, and substantial snowfall blanketed the vast stretches of countryside we traversed, obscuring our view of America's diverse landscapes. I vividly recall our passage through Salt Lake City, where everything appeared perpetually damp and gray beneath the winter sky. We reached Reno under the cover of darkness, but as we continued westward beyond the city limits, dawn broke, revealing a dramatically transformed landscape where the snow had vanished entirely. Upon entering the Sacramento Valley, we were greeted by a breathtaking landscape that seemed to herald our arrival in the promised land of California. The grass stretched endlessly in emerald waves, standing only a couple of feet tall, while countless peach trees displayed their magnificent spring blooms in delicate shades of pink, creating a pastoral panorama that filled us with wonder and anticipation.

The train eventually pulled into Oakland, and from there we took a boat to the Ferry Building in San Francisco, where representatives from the NCWC were waiting for us. They had been alerted to our arrival, and it was a pleasure to meet them. They suggested that since we had nearly the entire day before our departure, we might as well attend church, knowing that we were Catholics. They informed us there was a parish church just three blocks away and assured us we could easily walk there. Consequently, we stored our suitcases in a locker at the Ferry Building and set off on foot toward the church.

The Latin Mass provided a crucial anchor of familiarity in an otherwise bewildering new environment, demonstrating how religious traditions served as bridges between the old world and the new for Catholic immigrants. The universality of Latin liturgy meant that, despite being thousands of miles from home, the essential elements of worship remained comfortingly familiar. This spiritual continuity offered psychological stability during a period of profound transition, allowing us to maintain connection with our cultural identity even as everything else around us seemed foreign and challenging. The experience of attending Mass in San Francisco represented both an ending and a beginning—our last taste of European-style Catholicism before encountering the uniquely American expressions of faith that would shape our religious experience in the years to come.

After Mass, we still had quite some time before departing for Gustine, California, where our sponsor was. That day, March 3rd, was my friend, Peter's 20th birthday, while mine was still a month away, on April 8th. We decided to commemorate his birthday with two bottles of Coca-Cola from a vending machine, which we encountered for the very first time. We stood trans-fixed, watching how other people inserted coins into the mechanical contraption, and bottles of Coke miraculously dropped into the retrieval slot below. We mimicked their actions and successfully obtained two bottles of Coke, which we carried back to the Ferry Building. We also purchased some fresh bread, a substantial chunk of cheese, and one or two other modest provisions to celebrate Peter's milestone birthday in our own humble fashion.

The simple celebration of Peter's 20th birthday with Coca-Cola and cheese marked our first genuine taste of American consumer culture, symbolizing a transition from European emigrants to American consumers. The vending machine, a ubiquitous fixture of 1950s American convenience culture, embodied the technological innovation and automated efficiency that characterized American society. Our fascination with this mechanical marvel reflected the broader technological gap between post-war Europe and America, where such labor-saving devices were already becoming commonplace. The act of purchasing Coca-Cola—arguably America's most iconic beverage—served as an inadvertent initiation ritual into American commercial life, transforming us from bewildered foreigners into participating consumers in the American economy.

We had a lot of time on our hands, and we decided to go to a movie theater. It was also an opportunity to get out of the weather, which was not so good. We saw several movies, including one in color. That was the first time we saw a color movie. It was a wonderful experience for us.

We decided to explore the city through some leisurely sightseeing. We wandered the streets cautiously, always keeping visual contact with the Ferry Building, where our belongings were secured and from which we would eventually depart for our final destination. The weather proved typically San Franciscan—cold and uninviting, with an overcast sky and persistent drizzle. We wrapped ourselves tightly in our heavy overcoats to prevent getting thoroughly soaked.

We strolled the downtown streets, pressing our faces against store windows and marveling at the dazzling displays of American affluence that we had only heard described in stories from other emigrants. Later that night, our train crawled out of the station toward Gustine, our final destination.

The dramatic transformation of the landscape from the snow-covered Midwest to California's blooming valleys provided a powerful metaphor for the immigrant experience itself. The stark beauty of the Sacramento Valley, with its green grass and flowering peach trees, offered tangible evidence of the opportunities that had drawn millions of Europeans to American shores. This visual feast represented more than mere scenery—it was our first glimpse of California's agricultural abundance, the very industry that would provide our livelihood and shape our new identities as American farmers. The contrast between the harsh winter landscapes of the East and the spring-like promise of California reinforced our sense that we had made the right decision in leaving Holland, even as the language barrier and cultural uncertainties continued to loom large in our minds.

During the interminably slow train ride, with the train halting at virtually every station along the route, we grew increasingly anxious because we had no clear indication of when we would reach our designated stop. Consequently, I approached the conductor armed with a pocket dictionary and attempted to communicate our concerns as best I could. Through a combination of broken English, gestures, and persistent pointing at our destination written on paper, I managed to make him understand our predicament. He kindly reassured Peter and me not to worry and promised he would personally alert us when to disembark.

At long last, the conductor announced that the next stop was indeed ours. We hastily gathered our belongings, and when the train finally lurched to a halt, we stepped off into what appeared to be the middle of absolutely nowhere. The location could scarcely be dignified with the term "railway station," as it consisted of nothing more than a modest wooden platform where trains rarely stopped unless passengers specifically requested the conductor to make an unscheduled halt, exactly as we had done.

Remarkably, that modest town turned out to be our final destination. There we stood in the pitch darkness at two o'clock in the morning, disoriented and uncertain of our exact whereabouts. The silence of the sleeping town was broken only by the distant sound of the train that had brought us there as it pulled away into the night.

Suddenly, we spotted headlights cutting through the darkness, slowly approaching our location. Our hearts lifted with hope—surely this must be our sponsor coming to collect us. Instead, we found ourselves face-to-face with the local sheriff, whose patrol car came to a stop near where we stood with our luggage scattered around us. He had noticed the unscheduled train stop and grown curious about why the locomotive had paused in his quiet town at such an unusual hour, prompting him to investigate.

With nervous anticipation, we presented him with the envelope bearing our sponsor's name and address. Recognition dawned immediately across his weathered face. He explained that just a couple of weeks earlier, two other Dutch families and a young couple had arrived under similar circumstances, clutching identical envelopes and searching for the very same man. The sheriff's familiarity with the situation brought us immense relief.

Without hesitation, he escorted us to a modest hotel situated conveniently next to the police station. After rousing our sponsor from his sleep with a telephone call, the sheriff secured us a room for the remainder of the night. Exhausted from our long journey, we gratefully collapsed into real beds for the first time in what felt like an eternity.

The next morning brought our first face-to-face meeting with our sponsor, a kind-faced man who arrived promptly to collect us. He led us to a local restaurant where we experienced our first American breakfast—an array of unfamiliar dishes that would soon become routine. Communication was very difficult for Peter and me. I managed to catch a few scattered words here and there, but for the most part, we both relied on gestures, facial expressions, and educated guesswork to navigate our conversations.

After our meal, our sponsor drove us across town to meet the other Dutch families who had arrived several days earlier. These fellow immigrants had already begun the process of settling into their new lives, and their faces showed a mixture of recognition and sympathy as they saw fresh newcomers experiencing the same bewilderment they had recently endured. Our sponsor, speaking in halting Dutch phrases he had learned from the previous arrivals, asked these families to take us under their wing and help us locate suitable lodging in the community. Standing there among strangers who shared our homeland

and our circumstances, we felt the first glimmer of hope that we might truly be able to build a new life in this foreign place.

CHAPTER 7

Finding Our First Home

* * *

The Dutch families we met led us through the town's narrow streets to a small, weather-beaten house managed by a Portuguese woman whose English was only slightly better than our own. She operated what could generously be called a boarding house, renting individual rooms to four or five different tenants. The arrangement was simple but practical: everyone kept to their own space, sharing only the occasional nod of acknowledgment in the hallway.

We secured one of the available rooms, a sparse but clean space consisting of nothing more than a bedroom and a small bathroom. The furnishings were minimal—a bed, a single chair, and a small window that looked out onto the dusty street. After carefully unpacking our suitcases and arranging our meager possessions, we allowed ourselves a brief rest on the unfamiliar mattress. But restlessness soon overtook our fatigue, and we decided to venture out and explore our new surroundings.

The town revealed itself to be precisely what we had glimpsed in the darkness the night before—small, quiet, and utterly foreign to our European sensibilities. As we walked the main street, I realized we would need to establish some basic routines if we were going to function in this new environment. "Peter," I said, "if we're going to wake up early tomorrow morning for work, we need an alarm clock." The practicality of the statement struck us both—we were no longer travelers but residents, with responsibilities and schedules to keep.

We found a modest general store where a patient shopkeeper helped us select a reliable alarm clock, pointing to the numbers and miming the motion of winding it up. Communication remained a challenge, but basic transactions seemed manageable through gestures and pointing. Next, we located a small grocery store and methodically gathered the essentials for basic living: spoons, forks, knives, two plates, and some familiar foods like cereal and milk to serve as our first meals in our new home.

The Reality of Work

Our sponsor had arranged employment for us with a local farm operation, and the farm boss had been clear about expectations: his foreman would pick us up at precisely six o'clock the following morning. We set our new alarm clock with nervous anticipation, knowing it would mark the true beginning of our American working lives.

When the knock came at our door at exactly 6 a.m., we were dressed and ready, having woken several minutes before the alarm in our anxiety. The foreman, a weathered man who spoke in rapid, clipped sentences we couldn't fully understand, gestured for us to follow him to his truck.

The short drive took us to an expansive field stretching toward the horizon under the early-morning sky. What we encountered there was both reassuring and sobering: twenty-five other workers, representing what seemed like a small United Nations of recent immigrants. Men from Mexico worked alongside others from the Philippines, and we could hear fragments of various languages mixing in the morning air. All of them were engaged in the same backbreaking labor—digging into the hard-packed earth and methodically uprooting stubborn weeds that threatened the farm's crops.

As we took our places among this diverse workforce, the reality of our situation set in. This was no longer about surviving a journey or finding temporary shelter. This was the beginning of our new life as American workers, starting from the very bottom and working with our hands under the vast sky of our adopted homeland.

Learning Through Labor

Fortunately, Peter and I adapted quickly to the farm work. Having labored on farms back in Holland, we were no strangers to the rhythm of agricultural life—the early mornings, the methodical pace of weeding, and the satisfaction of working with our hands in the soil. The calluses on our palms had barely had time to soften during our journey, and we fell back into the familiar motions of hoeing and cultivating with relative ease.

However, our fellow Dutch immigrants presented a starkly different picture, and their struggles provided both sympathy and unintentional entertainment during those long working days. Among our group was a former Air Force pilot, a distinguished man who had commanded aircraft through the skies of Europe, now accompanied by his wife and two teenage daughters. None of them had ever performed manual labor of any kind—their soft hands and uncertain grips on the farming tools revealed their complete unfamiliarity with physical work.

Perhaps even more out of place was an accountant in his sixties who had spent decades managing finances for a major corporation. His careful, methodical nature served him well when working with numbers, but proved less useful when confronted with stubborn weeds and unforgiving soil. There was also a recent university graduate, bright and educated but utterly bewildered by the practical demands of farm labor—he held a hoe as if it were a foreign object, which in many ways, it was.

The fourth member of our Dutch contingent was a young man of about twenty-five who had spent several years working in a restaurant back home. While he understood hard work and long hours, the transition from serving customers indoors to battling weeds under the relentless California sun proved more challenging than he had anticipated.

Watching them navigate their first encounters with farm equipment provided moments of levity during otherwise grueling days. Many were seeing—let alone touching—such tools for the first time in their lives. The sight of the former pilot tentatively gripping a shovel, or the accountant puzzling over the proper angle for attacking a particularly stubborn weed, reminded us all of just how far we had traveled from our previous lives.

CHAPTER 8

Mount Arbor Farms and New Discoveries

* * *

Our workplace turned out to be quite impressive in scope. Our sponsor operated Mount Arbor Farms, a sprawling nursery specializing in rosebush cultivation that stretched across acres of California farmland. The main company headquarters, we learned, was located in Mount Arbor, Michigan, but they had established this West Coast operation specifically to take advantage of California's ideal climate for growing roses. The moderate temperatures, abundant sunshine, and controlled irrigation created perfect conditions for producing plants that would eventually grace gardens across America.

The scale of the operation gradually became apparent as we worked on different sections of the property. Row upon row of rose bushes in various stages of growth created a patchwork of green and color that extended far beyond what we could see from any single vantage point. It was, in its way, quite beautiful—even if our daily reality involved more weeding than flower appreciation.

Our introduction to the American financial system came with our first paycheck. It was a small amount because the rainy weather made it impossible for us to work all week. The cashier at the farm office, recognizing that we were recent immigrants struggling with the language, took extra care to explain as clearly as possible that we would need to visit a bank to convert this strange piece of paper into actual money. This represented our first encounter with the concept of a check—back in Holland, we had always been paid in cash, with physical money placed directly into our hands at the end of each work period.

The check itself seemed almost magical in its abstraction. Here was a small piece of paper that supposedly represented our week's wages, but we couldn't spend it anywhere until we performed some mysterious banking ritual. The cashier's patient explanations, supplemented by gestures and simplified English, gradually helped us understand the process.

We were also encouraged to open bank accounts, a concept that seemed both practical and slightly intimidating. The local Bank of America branch was indeed a modest establishment, fitting perfectly with the small-town atmosphere we were beginning to understand. Opening our savings accounts felt like crossing another threshold into American life—we were no longer just temporary visitors but people with official financial relationships in our new country.

Each month, we dutifully deposited small amounts from our paychecks, watching our savings grow with the satisfaction that comes from building something tangible for the future. After several months of this routine, we made a significant decision: it was time to purchase a car to get around town and reduce our dependence on others for transportation.

The Challenge of Getting a Driver's License

The automobile represented freedom and independence, but first, we had to navigate the bureaucratic maze of obtaining driver's licenses. Neither of us had this particular credential, which seemed essential to American life in a way it hadn't been in Holland. Our journey to the Department of Motor Vehicles office immediately highlighted our ongoing language difficulties. I had managed to pick up fragments of English and had developed the habit of carrying a small dictionary with me everywhere—it had become as essential as my wallet. Peter, however, remained almost entirely dependent on gestures and context clues to communicate.

When we arrived at the DMV, we discovered we had a choice between written and verbal examinations. This decision would prove more crucial than we initially understood. I inquired whether I could use my faithful dictionary as a reference during the written test, and to my relief, the answer was yes. Peter, perhaps intimidated by the prospect of reading English text, opted for the verbal examination.

The irony of our situation became apparent when the results were announced: I passed my test but had never actually learned to drive, while Peter failed his examination despite being a competent driver. We left the DMV that day with mixed feelings—progress had been made, but we were still far from our goal of automotive independence.

A week later, we returned for Peter's second attempt. This time, either through better preparation or simple luck, he managed to pass the verbal examination. We finally had the documentation required to legally operate a motor vehicle in California.

With our newly minted driver's licenses in hand, we set out to find our first American automobile. Our budget was modest, and we soon discovered a vehicle that seemed to fit our financial constraints: an older car priced at $300. The price seemed reasonable for our circumstances, and we eagerly completed the purchase, proud to have achieved this milestone of American independence.

Unfortunately, our celebration was short-lived. Within days of our purchase, we began to understand why the previous owner had been so willing to part with the vehicle at such an attractive price. The engine began to overheat with alarming regularity, turning even short trips around town into anxious adventures punctuated by roadside stops to let the motor cool down.

Our "bargain" had revealed itself to be anything but, serving as an expensive lesson in the reality that sometimes things appear too good to be true because they actually are. Nevertheless, even an unreliable car represented a form of progress, and we were determined to make the best of our situation while we saved money for something more dependable.

CHAPTER 9

The Call to Military Service

* * *

Our new life in America came with obligations we had not fully anticipated. One of the conditions attached to our immigration visas was a requirement that would fundamentally alter our immediate plans: we were obligated to report for military service after six months of residency. In 1957, as the specter of the Vietnam conflict loomed, this requirement carried weight far beyond a simple civic duty.

Neither Peter nor I had immigrated to America with any intention of participating in another war. We were still carrying the psychological scars of the devastation we had witnessed during World War II in Holland, and the prospect of being deployed to fight in a distant jungle conflict felt like a cruel irony. We had come to America to build something—specifically, we had dreams of establishing our own farm business, specializing in the cultivation and growing of flowers that would bring beauty rather than destruction into the world.

Fortunately, we discovered through conversations with other immigrants and residents that there was an alternative path. The National Guard offered a way to fulfill our military obligation while significantly reducing the likelihood of overseas deployment. This seemed like the perfect solution to our dilemma—we could satisfy the legal requirements of our visa status without abandoning our agricultural aspirations or risking involvement in active combat.

When our mandatory six-month waiting period concluded, we made our way to the National Guard recruitment office with a mixture of relief and apprehension. I was accepted into the program without difficulty, but Peter faced an unexpected obstacle: his considerable height disqualified him from service in both the regular army and the National Guard. Military regulations of the era apparently imposed strict limits on the physical dimensions of acceptable recruits, and Peter's stature exceeded those limits. This turn of events meant that while I would be fulfilling my military obligation, Peter would remain civilian.

Basic Training at Fort Ord

In March 1958, I reported to Fort Ord for six months of basic training, a journey that would prove to be one of the most challenging and transformative experiences of my American journey. The military had selected me to train as a medical corpsman, a designation that would provide me with valuable medical training.

The most immediate and overwhelming challenge I faced had nothing to do with physical fitness, military or discipline—it was the language barrier that nearly paralyzed me with fear. My English remained rudimentary at best, limited to basic phrases and heavily dependent on my ever-present dictionary. The prospect of navigating military training while barely able to express myself in the dominant language was not merely difficult; it was genuinely terrifying.

The drill sergeants, true to their reputation, communicated primarily through shouted commands delivered at a rapid-fire pace with military precision and absolutely no patience for confusion or hesitation. Finding myself surrounded by barking orders I could only partially comprehend while trying to execute unfamiliar movements and procedures created a stress that was almost unbearable during those first weeks.

However, I must acknowledge that military service provided an unexpected and invaluable benefit: it accelerated my English-language acquisition in ways that no classroom or textbook could have. During my months working in the agricultural fields alongside fellow immigrants from Latin America and the Philippines, I was surrounded by people who, like me, were struggling with English as a second language. While this created a comfortable, supportive environment, it also meant I had few opportunities to hear and practice conversational English.

The military environment forced me into constant interaction with native English speakers, requiring me to understand complex instructions, engage in conversations with fellow recruits, and express myself clearly enough to avoid potentially dangerous misunderstandings. The intensity and urgency of military training created a pressure-cooker environment for language learning that proved remarkably effective, even if it was often uncomfortable.

I celebrated my twenty-first birthday at Fort Ord. Among the recruits, conversation often turned to drinking habits, and I proudly declared that in Holland, we drank gin straight—no mixers, no fuss. My claim immediately aroused curiosity, and they challenged me to demonstrate this Dutch custom. With great ceremony, they poured a generous measure into a canteen cup and pushed it toward me.

I lifted the cup and took a confident swallow, determined to prove my point. But to my horror, the American gin tasted more like rubbing alcohol than anything I had ever encountered back home. It was sharp, raw, and altogether unpleasant. Still, I forced myself to drink it without so much as a grimace. The others watched me with wide eyes, waiting for some reaction, but to their surprise—and my quiet pride—it had little effect on me. If anything, the ordeal only confirmed for them that perhaps the Dutch really were made of sterner stuff.

Cultural Contrasts and War Memories

Beyond the language challenges, I found myself navigating significant cultural differences that highlighted just how far I had traveled from my European origins. Most of my fellow recruits were American-born young men, typically several years younger than I, who had grown up in a culture where firearms were commonplace. Many had been hunting since childhood, and virtually all of them had at least some familiarity with guns through family ownership or recreational shooting.

When I was issued my M1 rifle—a substantial, intimidating weapon that felt heavy and foreign in my hands—I experienced a wave of fear that my fellow soldiers could not have understood. This was not the nervousness of a novice handling his first firearm; this was the visceral reaction of someone who had witnessed firsthand what such weapons could do to human beings and entire communities. The weight of the rifle in my hands immediately transported me back to the darkest days of the war in Holland, when similar weapons had brought nothing but death and destruction to our homeland.

During the first few weeks of training, the military showed us numerous war films designed to build esprit de corps and prepare us psychologically for potential combat situations. These Hollywood productions, with their dramatic music, heroic narratives, and sanitized violence, struck me as almost absurdly disconnected from reality. When my fellow recruits became excited or inspired by these cinematic depictions of warfare, I felt compelled to offer a different perspective.

"Even though I had never held a weapon before coming here," I would tell them during our evening conversations, "what you're seeing in those movies is nothing strange to me. I have lived through a real war—not a fictionalized Hollywood version—and let me tell you, the reality is nothing like what they show on screen." These conversations often led to sobering discussions about the true cost of conflict, and I hope they gave my younger colleagues a more realistic understanding of what military service might ultimately entail.

Advanced Training in Texas

Perhaps most importantly, this period underscored the critical need to respect the military chain of command. We learned to follow orders without question, to trust our superiors' decision-making, and to understand our place within the larger military hierarchy. For someone who had spent his adult life making independent decisions as a farmer and immigrant, this aspect of military culture required a significant psychological adjustment.

The Texas training environment posed unique challenges, from the oppressive heat and humidity that made every outdoor exercise an endurance test to the cultural differences I encountered among recruits from across the American South and Southwest. Nevertheless, by the time I completed this phase of my service, I had developed not only the technical skills required of a medical corpsman but also a much deeper understanding of American culture, vastly improved English language abilities, and a network of friendships that would prove valuable in the years to come.

The irony was not lost on me that military service—something I had initially viewed as an unwelcome obligation that might derail my agricultural dreams—had provided me with tools and experiences that would prove invaluable in building my American life.

CHAPTER 10

Assignment to the 149th Artillery Battalion

* * *

Following my completion of training, I received orders to report to my permanent National Guard unit: the 149th Anti-Aircraft Artillery Battalion, stationed in San Mateo. This assignment would determine how I would spend my remaining military obligation while continuing to build my civilian life in California.

The 149th was a substantial operation, but their medical detachment consisted of only a handful of personnel—far fewer than the unit's size would normally warrant. The commanding officers had identified this shortage and determined that my recent medical corpsman training made me an ideal candidate to fill the gap. While I felt somewhat apprehensive about the responsibility, I was also grateful to be placed in a role that aligned with my training and, more importantly, with my values of helping rather than harming others.

The medical detachment assignment proved to be another crucial milestone in my English language development. There's something remarkable about how quickly linguistic barriers dissolve when communication becomes a matter of life and death. When you're responsible for understanding medical procedures, following emergency protocols, and potentially treating injured soldiers, academic language learning transforms into an urgent necessity.

Although I still struggled with spoken English and often felt self-conscious about my accent and limited vocabulary, I discovered that reading and comprehending written instructions presented far fewer challenges. Medical terminology, with its Latin roots and systematic structure, actually proved more accessible than casual conversation. The technical nature of our training materials, combined with the disciplined approach of military instruction, created a learning environment that suited my practical, detail-oriented mindset.

My fellow medical personnel were remarkably patient and supportive, recognizing that effective teamwork required clear communication from everyone involved. They took the time to explain procedures slowly, demonstrated techniques repeatedly when necessary, and created an atmosphere in which asking questions was encouraged rather than criticized. The fundamental nature of our training—focused on essential, life-saving skills rather than complex theoretical concepts—also worked in my favor.

Medical Training and Responsibilities

Our medical education covered a comprehensive range of essentials in battlefield medicine. We learned basic first aid procedures that could mean the difference between life and death in emergencies. More specifically, we studied techniques for treating soldiers wounded in combat: how to quickly assess injuries, properly bandage various types of wounds, create effective splints for broken bones, and safely evacuate injured personnel from dangerous field conditions.

As our training progressed, we advanced to more sophisticated medical support operations. We learned the intricate process of establishing field hospitals, including the proper set-up of medical tents that could function effectively in various weather conditions and terrain. Perhaps most challenging, we trained to assist surgeons during field operations, learning to anticipate their needs, maintain sterile conditions under difficult circumstances, and provide critical support during life-saving procedures.

Our medical education also included the basics of pharmacology—understanding essential medications, their proper dosages, and safe administration methods. This knowledge was crucial for providing immediate care before more advanced medical help could arrive, and it required memorizing information that could prove vital in high-stress situations.

Our medical detachment operated under the supervision of our own captain, a qualified doctor who provided both medical expertise and military leadership. Having a physician as our commanding officer created an environment in which medical considerations received appropriate priority and our training remained focused on practical, clinically sound procedures rather than purely military protocol.

The National Guard structure required ongoing training commitments that extended well beyond our initial preparation. Each summer, we participated in intensive two-week training exercises that took us to military installations throughout California, including extended periods at Camp Roberts and Hunter Liggett Military Reservation. These exercises served multiple purposes: they maintained our readiness for potential deployment, provided opportunities to practice our skills in realistic field conditions, and fostered unit cohesion among personnel who spent most of the year in civilian occupations.

Field Exercises and Real-World Application

During major training operations, our role shifted from classroom learning to practical field medicine. While the main artillery units conducted their combat exercises—practicing with the heavy weapons and sophisticated equipment that defined their military mission—we served as their essential safety net. Our responsibility was to provide immediate medical response for any training injuries, equipment accidents, or health emergencies that might occur during these intensive exercises.

These field deployments required us to establish fully functional medical stations in temporary locations, often under challenging conditions. We had to transport all necessary medical supplies, set up treatment areas that met both medical and military standards, and maintain constant readiness to respond to emergencies. The work was physically demanding and mentally taxing, but it provided invaluable experience in working under pressure while applying our medical training in realistic scenarios.

The responsibility of ensuring the safety and well-being of fellow soldiers during training exercises gave our work a sense of purpose that transcended routine military duty. We weren't simply fulfilling an obligation or completing training requirements—we were providing an essential service that could prevent serious injuries from becoming life-threatening emergencies. This understanding transformed what could have been tedious military service into meaningful work that directly aligned with my fundamental values of helping others and contributing positively to my community.

Transition to Artillery Operations

During my final two years of National Guard service, the military underwent one of its periodic reorganizations that would fundamentally change my role and responsibilities. The 149th unit was converted from an anti-aircraft artillery battalion to a conventional artillery unit, eliminating the need for specialized medical detachments. Rather than transferring me to another medical unit, the commanding officers decided to retrain me for direct artillery operations.

My new assignment was as a forward observer, a position that required a completely different skill set from medical work but proved equally fascinating in its own way. The role of a forward observer is both critical and dangerous: while the main artillery crews operate their guns from protected positions several miles behind the front lines, forward observers must position themselves much closer to enemy territory—often on exposed hilltops or other elevated positions—where they can directly observe the impact of artillery shells and provide real-time targeting adjustments.

This work demanded a unique combination of courage, mathematical precision, and communication skills. Using powerful binoculars and other optical equipment, I would watch artillery rounds impact in the target area, then quickly calculate the necessary adjustments to bring subsequent rounds precisely on target. The calculations involved understanding trajectory, wind conditions, distance, and elevation changes—mathematical concepts that challenged my mind in ways different from those in my medical training.

The responsibility was both exhilarating and sobering. Artillery pieces can deliver devastating firepower across enormous distances, but their effectiveness depends entirely on accurate targeting information from forward observers. A miscalculation or miscommunication could mean the difference between hitting an enemy position and causing friendly fire casualties.

During training exercises, I also had the opportunity to operate the artillery pieces and actually fire rounds during practice sessions. There's something simultaneously thrilling and intimidating about triggering the release of such enormous, destructive power. The ground-shaking roar of the guns, the smell of gunpowder, and the visible flash of muzzle fire created sensory experiences unlike anything I had encountered in civilian life.

Despite my earlier fears about handling weapons, I found the technical aspects of artillery work genuinely engaging. The precision required, the mathematical calculations, and the teamwork necessary to coordinate effective fire missions appealed to my systematic, detail-oriented nature.

The Rhythm of Military Life

My National Guard service settled into a predictable but demanding routine that shaped my life for several years. Once a month, I reported for Monday evening training sessions that typically ran late into the night, covering everything from equipment maintenance to tactical procedures. Additionally, one full

Sunday each month was dedicated to more intensive training exercises, often involving field maneuvers.

The most significant commitment came annually during the summer training period—two full weeks away from civilian life and business responsibilities. These exercises invariably took me to Camp Roberts for the first week, followed by another week of field operations in the surrounding hills and valleys. The proximity of Hunter Liggett Military Reservation, located just behind Camp Roberts in the rugged coastal mountains, made logistics convenient, as all our training could be conducted within a relatively compact area.

However, the convenience of nearby training facilities was offset by the considerable distance between the military base and my home in Half Moon Bay. The geography of California's Central Coast meant that what appeared to be neighboring regions on a map actually required hours of travel across mountain ranges and through varying climate zones.

I'll never forget one particularly striking weekend during the first two weeks of June when the contrast between California's microclimates was dramatically illustrated. We had been training in the inland valleys around Camp Roberts, where summer temperatures regularly soared well above 100 degrees. On this particular Saturday afternoon, as we prepared to depart for a brief weekend leave, the thermometer registered 111 degrees in the shade—heat so intense that even standing under trees provided little relief.

Most weekends during annual training, we remained on base, but this particular weekend, several units were granted leave to return home, partly because some needed to collect additional equipment or handle personal matters that couldn't wait. I was fortunate to secure a ride in a military truck heading toward the Bay Area, a road trip that would take us three to four hours through California's diverse landscape.

As we began our drive northwards, the oppressive inland heat made every mile feel interminable. The truck's metal surfaces were too hot to touch, and even with windows down, the rushing air provided little cooling relief.

We arrived at the armory in San Mateo, where I had packed my pickup truck. I then drove to my home in Half Moon Bay. Halfway through my trip, as I headed westward through the coastal mountain passes, I found the need to use my windshield wipers—not because of rain, but because of the dense fog that had begun to envelop my truck. By the time I reached Half Moon Bay, the temperature had dropped nearly fifty degrees, and the cool, misty air felt like entering a different world entirely. The contrast was so dramatic that it seemed almost impossible we had started our trip in such brutal heat just hours earlier.

That night, despite my exhaustion from the week's training, I slept best because of the cool weather. Whether it was the dramatic temperature change, the excitement of being home, or simply the knowledge that I would have to return to Camp Roberts the following evening, acutely aware that this brief respite would end all too soon.

Reflecting on Military Service

Looking back on my National Guard experience, I can honestly say that despite my initial reluctance and fears, the service provided me with invaluable opportunities for personal growth and development. The language skills I acquired proved essential to my future business success, but the benefits extended far beyond mere communication.

The military taught me discipline, punctuality, and attention to detail that served me well in civilian life. I learned to work effectively as part of a team, to follow complex instructions precisely, and to remain calm under pressure—skills that would prove crucial when Peter and I eventually started our own business. Perhaps most importantly, the service expanded my horizons and exposed me to experiences I never would have encountered in my previous agricultural work.

For someone who had received limited formal education in Holland and had little exposure to technical or mechanical subjects, the military training represented a comprehensive education in itself. I learned about equipment maintenance, logistics, communication systems, and problem-solving techniques that broadened my understanding of how complex organizations function effectively.

Building a Life and Family

* * *

One of my first and most important decisions was to marry Martha, the wonderful woman I had met in the greenhouse whose warmth and laughter had brightened my days throughout my military service. We discovered we had much in common beyond our immigrant status—similar values, dreams for the future, and a deep appreciation for the opportunities America offered. After a couple of years of courtship, we decided to take the next step and get married. We tied the knot on November 26, 1960, and followed with the beginnings of our own new family.

I built my first set of greenhouses in 1959, and just before we got married, I finished my second set. We thought this would give us enough income to get married. However, on November 13, 1959, barely weeks before our wedding, I received news that a tornado had swept through the area and destroyed my greenhouses. I was in military training, and when I came back,

I found that all my greenhouses had been completely damaged. My neighbors and other nursery farmers in the area came to my aid, and we were able to rebuild in time for me to harvest flowers there for our wedding.

We didn't have much family. Martha's uncle and a few nieces were present. There was no one from my family, except my friend, Peter, who served as my best man. We were married in Saint Bruno Catholic Church in San Bruno, on the San Francisco Peninsula.

From our wedding, we got only a few pictures, just about a dozen pictures. Cameras were not as common in those days as they are today, and when available, camera owners always charged an arm and a leg. Our wedding marked not just a personal milestone, but the beginning of the family we would build together in our adopted homeland.

Martha, who was also an immigrant from El Salvador, arrived in this country in 1956, a year before I made my journey from the Netherlands. We both found ourselves working at the same nursery in South San Francisco, where we spent our days tending to plants and gradually getting to know each other. The shared experience of being newcomers to America and working side by side in the greenhouse created a natural bond between us.

After Martha and I married, and had been in the United States for just about five years, we were eligible for citizenship—a milestone that felt truly amazing to us. Martha and I were keenly aware that we were El Salvadoran and Dutch citizens, respectively, and that our young children would be born as American citizens. For several years, we had the remarkable situation of three different nationalities represented in one family, sitting around our kitchen table each evening. This kind of multicultural blend within a single household represents something uniquely special about America—the way different cultures can come together and create something entirely new and beautiful while still honoring their respective origins.

Challenging Early Marriage Years

Life in those early years of our marriage was very difficult as we struggled to make ends meet. We established our home in Half Moon Bay, a coastal community south of San Francisco that offered the perfect combination of agricultural opportunities and natural beauty. This picturesque town, with its fog-shrouded mornings, fertile farmland, and proximity to both the ocean and major markets, would become the setting for the most important chapters of our American story.

The business my friend, Peter, and I had started was not yet generating much income, and we lived paycheck to paycheck, wondering if our entrepreneurial gamble would ever pay off. We didn't have any income from the business until about a year later—yes, that's when we started selling our first flowers. The moment we made that first sale was pretty exciting, marking the beginning of what would become our life's work. We started little by little, building our customer base one bouquet at a time, learning the intricacies of the flower business through trial and error. Those challenging beginnings notwithstanding, we still ran the business together for 40 years.

Over the years, our family grew to include six children, each born and raised as proud Americans while maintaining an appreciation for their diverse heritage. We named our first daughter Betsy. A year and a half later, we had another daughter, Alice, followed by another, Nancy. After our daughters, we had two sons: the elder, Albert and the younger, Edward. Our sons were followed by our last daughter, named Carla. All our children were born in Half Moon Bay, where we lived for 38 years.

Half Moon Bay provided an ideal environment for raising a family—safe neighborhoods and a close-knit community where everyone knew their neighbors. Watching our children grow up as native English speakers, fully integrated into American culture while respecting their parents' immigrant journey, gave us tremendous satisfaction and confirmed that our decision to come to America had been the right one.

After Edward was born, we realized we needed a new home with enough room for everyone. So, we went house-hunting and found a house large enough for one family, but the cost was higher than we could afford. It was then that one of our flower buyers, Charlie Levarone, offered to help us with a down payment. He said, "Pay it back whenever you can. If I don't let you have it, the money will just be sitting idly in the bank, anyway. So I might as well let you have it." That's how we were able to make a down payment for our home. What a noble man, Charlie was! Generous with his time, and even more generous with his money.

Educational Opportunities for our Children

One problem we had with our children was that they all needed braces, which were not cheap. I guess they all inherited their bad teeth from me, but the cost of fixing them was huge. Our two boys had problems learning in public school, so we sent them to a private school, which was quite expensive. After high school, all the kids went to college, which was also expensive. I didn't have much of an education in Holland, growing up during the war years when schools were shut down toward the end of the war, and survival took precedence over learning. School was free from kindergarten through 8th grade. After turning 15, I left school and started working. That painful experience is why, when I got married and began raising a family, Martha and I decided to save as much money as possible and ensure that our children had the kind of education we couldn't have. Growing up in El Salvador, she didn't have much of an education either because of the poor conditions her family lived in.

We made countless sacrifices, often going without luxuries and working extra hours to build their college funds. It was not easy because sometimes we had three of them in college at the same time, which was a tremendous financial burden that stretched our resources to the limit. But every penny was worth it when we saw them walk across those graduation stages. Now they have grown up, established themselves in successful careers, and can take care of themselves financially and emotionally, and that's truly a blessing that fills us with pride every day.

Our educational legacy began with our first daughter, Betsy, who graduated as a registered nurse from the University of San Francisco, launching a healthcare career that allowed her to serve others while achieving financial independence and professional respect. She later met someone special, a police officer in Oakland, and they got married. After retiring from active duty, they moved to Montana, where they still live. The distance meant we wouldn't see them as frequently as we might have liked, but we were happy that she had found love and was building her own life in a place that suited her and her husband's aspirations.

Our second daughter, Alice, graduated from Santa Clara University, where she studied computer science during the early years of the technology boom. Her technical education led to an exciting career as a software engineer for a contractor at NASA Ames Research Center for several years and for Oracle in Redwood Shores, California, before she made the personal decision to leave her career to focus on raising her own children. She got married and settled in Gilroy, California.

Our third daughter, Nancy, graduated from the University of California, Davis, with a Bachelor of Science degree in Agricultural Science and Management. She worked for the County of San Mateo Department of Agriculture as a Biologist/Standards Specialist for many years. She also found her life partner, a commercial fisherman. They got married, settled in Half Moon Bay, and we sold them the same home we had lived in during our flower-growing years, the one where Martha had endured all those foggy, cold mornings. The location turned out to be perfect for our son-in-law's fishing profession, as the house was situated close to the harbor, providing him with convenient access to the water and adequate space along the waterfront to dock and maintain his boats. This arrangement worked out exceptionally well for everyone involved—they got a home in an ideal location for his fishing pursuits, we were able to keep the property within the family, and we had one less thing to worry about as we settled into our new life in Templeton.

Both of our sons, Albert and Edward, followed similar paths to higher education, graduating from California Polytechnic State University San Luis Obispo, commonly known as Cal Poly, where they pursued degrees in agriculture. Through the years, Albert found himself working as the State Agronomist of Nevada and ultimately as a district conservationist for the US Department of Agriculture Natural Resources Conservation Service. He lives in Nevada with his family. Edward became a paramedic and managed a successful yogurt side business at Avila Beach, CA. At present, he works as a hospital radiologic technologist on the central coast of California.

Our youngest daughter, Carla, perhaps traveled the farthest for her education, graduating from the University of Washington in Seattle, Washington, where she completed her undergraduate studies in a program that prepared her for advanced professional training. Not satisfied with just one degree, she pursued her passion for animal care by enrolling in the highly competitive veterinary science program at the University of California, Davis, one of the nation's top veterinary schools. Her dedication to completing this demanding course of study represents the culmination of our family's commitment to education and professional achievement.

The success of all six of our children in completing their college education and establishing successful careers stands as perhaps our greatest achievement as parents. Each degree represents not just individual accomplishment, but the realization of dreams that Martha and I held during those challenging early years when we worked long hours in the flower business and saved every possible penny for their future education.

We have been very fortunate in many ways, watching our children become responsible adults who contribute positively to society. Now our children have their own children, and we are now grandparents to eight wonderful grandchildren who bring great joy to our lives. It is always a delight to help them from time to time with their kids or other chores around their homes, especially for those who live nearby, where we can be more hands-on. Every Thanksgiving, Christmas, and a couple of other times throughout the year, the whole family makes an effort to reunite, and those gatherings are filled with laughter, storytelling, and the kind of warmth that makes all the years of hard work feel meaningful. The house fills with the sounds of children playing and adults catching up, creating memories that sustain us throughout the year until we can all be together again.

CHAPTER 12

Entrepreneurial Beginnings

* * *

Peter and I took what was to be our biggest leap of hope. We launched our flower-growing business in 1959, just two years after our arrival in America, when we discovered several acres of suitable land available for rent in Half Moon Bay. Drawing on our horticultural background and the experience we gained working at various nurseries, we established a flower-growing operation that would become our life's work. The timing felt right—we had gained enough experience working for other nurseries to understand the basics of the industry, and we had saved enough money to make a modest start.

Even though our initial investment consisted of just a couple of hundred dollars, an amount that was barely sufficient to cover the most basic greenhouse operations, our business proved remarkably successful, lasting for four decades and providing not only financial security for our families but also the deep satisfaction that comes from building something meaningful with your own hands. We specialized in cut flowers, developing expertise in cultivation techniques that allowed us to compete effectively in California's demanding agricultural market.

We owed our long-term success to several factors: our genuine love for growing things, our willingness to work incredibly long hours, our attention to quality that reflected our European training, and our gradual mastery of American business practices. Over the years, we expanded our operations, developed relationships with wholesale buyers throughout the region, and built a reputation for reliability and excellence that sustained us through economic downturns and seasonal fluctuations. What had seemed like an almost impossible aspiration when we stood in that government office in Holland had transformed into a thriving enterprise that supported multiple families and contributed to our community's economic vitality.

The beginning was far from glamorous, though. We purchased essential equipment secondhand, constructed simple growing structures ourselves, and approached every expense with the careful consideration that comes from having very little margin for error. Those early months and years required tremendous sacrifice from both of us. Peter maintained his regular job to ensure we had a reliable income to cover basic living expenses, while I focused primarily on developing our growing operations. We essentially survived on his modest salary while reinvesting every penny of flower sales back into expanding our capabilities.

We also bought machines from Holland: bulb-sorting machines, grading and bunching machines. They counted the flowers in bunches of ten and tied them up for sale. We were young—barely twenty-one years old—and neither of us was married at the time, partly because we simply couldn't afford to support families on our meager income. This period of our lives required us to live extremely frugally, sharing expenses and postponing many of the pleasures and comforts that we hoped to enjoy once our business became established.

Despite the financial challenges, there was something thrilling about building our own enterprise from nothing. Every flower we successfully grew and sold represented tangible progress toward our American dream. We worked incredibly long hours, learned from our mistakes, and gradually developed the expertise and reputation that would eventually transform our modest beginning into a thriving forty-year enterprise.

The combination of our European horticultural background, our American work ethic, and our determination to succeed created a foundation for business success that would support our families for decades to come. What began as a desperate attempt to establish financial independence eventually became a source of great pride and accomplishment—proof that with enough dedication and hard work, even the humblest beginnings could lead to remarkable outcomes.

The situation with the land we leased in Miramar, a small town a few miles north of Half Moon Bay, was becoming increasingly problematic. Since it was leased property, we had no long-term security or ability to make permanent improvements. Recognizing that we needed to establish a more stable foundation for our growing business, we made a significant decision in 1960 to purchase six acres of agricultural land in Pescadero, California. This investment represented a major step forward in our entrepreneurial journey, as we now owned the land outright and could build permanent structures on it and plan for long-term expansion.

On this new property, we constructed multiple greenhouses from the ground up, creating a proper commercial flower-growing operation. However, we weren't ready to abandon our Miramar location immediately, as it was still productive and we had existing contracts to fulfill. For several more years, we maintained both operations simultaneously, continuing to cultivate flowers at the Miramar lease while developing our new Pescadero facility. This dual-location approach allowed us to gradually transition our business while maximizing our production capacity during the peak growing seasons.

Our operation was particularly noteworthy because we specialized in importing high-quality plants directly from Holland, leveraging my connections and knowledge of the Dutch horticultural industry. We became pioneers in American agriculture as the first farmers to successfully cultivate Alstroemeria on a commercial scale in the United States. These beautiful, long-lasting flowers, also known as Peruvian lilies, were relatively unknown in the American market at the time, but we recognized their commercial potential and invested heavily in perfecting the growing techniques needed to produce them reliably in California's climate.

True to our entrepreneurial spirit and our desire to control costs, we handled virtually every aspect of the operation ourselves, contracting outside assistance only when we absolutely couldn't manage a task on our own. We built all the greenhouses with our own hands, learning construction techniques as we went. We installed all the plumbing systems needed for irrigation and drainage of our flower beds, and wired all the electrical installations required for heating, lighting, and ventilation. This do-it-yourself approach was born partly out of necessity—we simply couldn't afford to hire contractors for every job—but it also reflected our work ethic and determination to master every aspect of our business.

This hands-on approach proved to be one of the most important factors in our eventual success, as it saved us enormous amounts of money that would otherwise have gone to outside contractors and specialists. Every dollar we saved on construction and installation could be reinvested in seeds, equipment, or expanding our growing capacity. Additionally, by intimately understanding every system in our operation, we could quickly diagnose and fix problems as they arose, minimizing downtime and crop losses.

Fortunately, our timing in entering the commercial flower market proved to be excellent. Flower prices were relatively high during this period, and demand was strong from florists and retailers throughout the San Francisco Bay Area and beyond. Business was good, and we began to see real financial returns on our investment and hard work.

However, this success came at a personal cost. Even though we were now operating full-time in Pescadero, I was still living with my family in Half Moon Bay. I had to commute to work every day, typically leaving home by six o'clock in the morning, arriving at the farm in time to begin the day's work, and rarely returning home before eight in the evening. This grueling schedule, which I maintained six days a week, began to take a noticeable toll on my family life. I found myself with precious little time to spend with my children during their waking hours, missing dinners, bedtime stories, and the countless small moments that make up the fabric of family life.

Recognizing this problem, I tried to make the most of whatever opportunities I could find to include my children in my work life. Whenever possible, especially on Saturdays, when the pace was somewhat less frantic, I would bring my kids to the farm. These Saturday visits served multiple purposes: they allowed me to spend time with my children while still attending to necessary farm work, they gave my kids an understanding of how their father earned the family's living, and they provided valuable lessons about work ethic, responsibility, and the satisfaction that comes from growing things.

Meanwhile, my friend Peter, who was still living in San Mateo, faced an even longer daily commute to reach our Pescadero operation. Despite the distance and travel time involved, Peter was reluctant to relocate his family closer to the farm, preferring to maintain his established life in San Mateo.

We occasionally involved our children in our flower business by having them clean flower bulbs and paying them for each box they completed. Both Peter and I would bring flower bulbs home for our children to clean. We believed strongly in teaching our children the value of work, so we made it a point to compensate them fairly for their contributions to the farm operation. By paying them for their efforts, we helped them understand that honest work has real value and that contributing to the family business was both a responsibility and an opportunity to earn their own money.

Martha never truly felt comfortable living in Half Moon Bay, and I completely understood her feelings. Having grown up in El Salvador, a warm tropical country blessed with consistent sunshine and moderate year-round temperatures, she found the stark contrast between Half Moon Bay's perpetually cold, foggy climate difficult to endure. The marine layer that rolled in from the Pacific Ocean seemed to blanket our town in gray mist for much of the year, creating a damp chill that penetrated right to the bones. For someone accustomed to the vibrant warmth and tropical weather of Central America, this relentless coastal weather felt oppressive and depressing. Recognizing her unhappiness and wanting to honor her feelings, I made her a heartfelt promise: if we ever left the flower business and had the financial freedom to relocate, we would move to a more agreeable climate.

It was during this period that our family was struck by a devastating tragedy that would change everything. My dear friend and business partner Peter's oldest son, Nick, died in a horrific airplane crash that claimed the lives of all passengers aboard. He was an exceptional young man—even taller than his already tall father—and had distinguished himself as a talented basketball player throughout his school years. His athletic prowess had earned him a college scholarship, and after graduation, his skills were good enough to earn him a professional basketball contract with the Phoenix Suns. The kid had genuine talent and a bright future ahead of him in professional sports.

On that fateful day, he and his girlfriend were returning from Detroit, Michigan, to Phoenix, Arizona, when the aircraft they were traveling in, a Northwest Airlines plane, encountered a catastrophic problem and crashed, killing everyone on board instantly. The news hit us like a physical blow. It was really tough for Peter and his entire family, who were devastated by the sudden loss of their eldest son and brother. My family was also greatly affected by this loss, as our two families were running the flower business together. The young man's sudden death touched all of us profoundly.

Opting out of the business

As time passed, Peter's second son, Peter Junior, graduated from college and expressed interest in joining our flower business full-time. I gave this proposition serious thought, considering all the implications and potential complications. The more I analyzed the situation, the more I realized that it would create an inherently difficult dynamic. There would be two family members from Peter's side working in the business, while I would remain the only representative of my family actively involved in day-to-day operations. This imbalance could lead to disagreements over business decisions, profit-sharing, and long-term planning. I could foresee situations where father and son might naturally align on one side of an issue, leaving me in a minority position despite being an equal partner.

When I shared these concerns with Peter, he remained enthusiastic about having his son join the business and seemed confident that we could make it work. However, I felt that the fairest solution for everyone involved would be a clean break. I proposed that if he was determined to bring his son into the operation, perhaps they should buy out my entire share of the business. This would give them complete control over their family enterprise while providing me with the capital I needed to pursue other opportunities and fulfill my promise to Martha about leaving Half Moon Bay.

The buyout negotiations proved to be complex and emotionally charged, lasting nearly two years as we worked through the details of valuing our joint assets, determining fair compensation for the business we had built together, and handling the legal aspects of dissolving our partnership. These discussions sometimes strained our friendship, as business negotiations often do, but we both remained committed to reaching an agreement that felt fair to both families. Finally, after months of back-and-forth discussions with attorneys and accountants, we agreed on a purchase price that reflected the true value of what we had created together. On January 1, 1997, I officially left the flower business, turning over my share of the operation to Peter and his son.

The business still exists today, but it's struggling because the floral industry has changed dramatically, with big-box stores and online retailers dominating the market. Local flower farms, like ours, face challenges that didn't exist when we started. I got out pretty much at the right time. The industry was shifting in ways that would make it difficult for small, family-owned businesses to compete. That transition happened in 1997, marking the end of an era for both Martha and me.

Membership of the Farm Bureau

One of my most treasured experiences was my deep involvement with the San Mateo County Farm Bureau, an organization that became central to both my professional development and personal fulfillment as an agricultural advocate. My commitment to the Bureau spanned decades, during which I had the profound honor of serving as president from 1966 to 1968—a role that allowed me to champion the interests of local farmers during a transformative period in California agriculture.

The recognition I received from my fellow farmers meant more to me than any other professional accolade. Being named Farmer of the Year not once, but twice—first in 1988 and again in 1995—represented validation from peers who understood the daily challenges, seasonal uncertainties, and unwavering dedication that farming demands. These awards weren't just personal achievements; they reflected my commitment to advancing sustainable agricultural practices and fostering collaboration within our farming community.

During my tenure as president, I witnessed firsthand how the Farm Bureau served as both advocate and educator, bridging the gap between rural agricultural needs and urban policy decisions. The relationships I built through this organization—with fellow farmers, agricultural researchers, and community leaders—enriched my understanding of farming not just as a livelihood but as stewardship of the land and service to the broader community.

My involvement with the San Mateo County Farm Bureau remains one of the defining chapters of my life, representing years of meaningful service, professional growth, and the deep satisfaction that comes from contributing to something larger than oneself.

CHAPTER 13

We Moved out of Half Moon Bay

* * *

With the business sold and the promise I had made to Martha finally within reach, I told her that her long-cherished wish to leave Half Moon Bay was now fulfilled. We began searching for a new home in a warmer, sunnier location and eventually decided on Templeton, California, a charming small town near Paso Robles in San Luis Obispo County. The area offered the kind of climate Martha had been longing for—warm, dry summers and mild winters with plenty of sunshine year-round, a dramatic improvement over the perpetual fog of the coast.

We purchased a house that was significantly larger than our previous home in Half Moon Bay, which proved to be fortunate timing because we needed the extra space for a very important reason. Martha's elderly mother had moved in with us from El Salvador following the death of her husband. The poor woman was already well advanced in years, did not speak a single word of English, and was beginning to show signs of dementia that made it impossible for her to live independently. When we designed and built our new house in Templeton, we made special provision for her needs by creating a comfortable private room equipped with everything she needed to maintain her dignity and comfort.

This arrangement worked out well for our entire family. Martha's mother lived with us for over twenty years, during which time we provided her with the care, love, and support she needed during her declining years. When she finally passed away peacefully, we honored her memory and Martha's cultural traditions by transporting her mortal remains back to El Salvador, where she was laid to rest beside her beloved husband in their homeland. Remarkably, her death occurred in 2005, exactly 9 years after we had made our own life-changing move away from Half Moon Bay, marking the end of one chapter in our family's story and the beginning of another.

Our new home sat just a few miles from Camp Roberts and Hunter Liggett Military Reservation—the very training grounds where I had spent those memorable summers during my National Guard service decades earlier. This geographic proximity created an unexpected connection to my military past that I never could have anticipated when choosing our retirement location.

Every summer, when current National Guard units arrive for their annual training exercises, the sound of artillery fire echoes across the hills and valleys of San Luis Obispo County. These distant thunder-like rumbles always transported me back to those challenging but formative years when I was learning to be both an American and a soldier. The sounds that once filled me with anxiety and reminded me of wartime trauma in

Holland now evoked different memories—recollections of personal growth, language acquisition, teamwork, and the gradual transformation from a frightened immigrant to a confident American citizen.

Sitting on my porch in Templeton, listening to those familiar sounds of military training, I was always struck by the remarkable journey that brought me from my war-torn Twello to a successful American business and family life. Each artillery round echoing in the distance served as a reminder not just of my military service, but of the unexpected pathways that led to a life far more prosperous and more fulfilling than anything I could have imagined when I first stepped off that train in the California darkness so many years earlier.

The circle of my American story feels remarkably complete: from a fearful immigrant to a successful businessman; from a struggling non-English speaker to a confident community member, from a reluctant soldier to a proud veteran—all while building a family and business that represent the very best of what America can offer to those willing to work for their dreams.

CHAPTER 14

The Long-Awaited Visit

* * *

Now that I had effectively taken leave of the farm, I was ready to rest and do what I couldn't do when Peter and I owned the farm. I could now turn my full attention to my family. We could now travel, see, and visit places we couldn't go to in the past. When we got married, we started having children almost immediately, which naturally curtailed our ability to travel as much as we would have loved. The responsibilities of raising a growing family, combined with the financial demands of diapers, baby formula, medical expenses, and other costs of raising young children, made international travel seem like an impossible luxury. Besides, traveling overseas is not cheap under any circumstances, but especially challenging when you're considering airline tickets, accommodations, and meals for multiple family members. The cost of flying even one or two people to

Europe in those days represented a significant portion of our annual income, let alone the expense of taking an entire family.

That financial reality, combined with the practical challenges of traveling with small children, meant it took me almost 20 years to return for a visit after I left Holland. Those two decades felt like both an eternity and a brief moment—an eternity because I missed my family and homeland deeply, yet brief because the years flew by in the whirlwind of establishing our business, raising our children, and building our life in America. During those years, I stayed connected with my family through letters and occasional phone calls, but the ocean between us felt vast and sometimes insurmountable.

The opportunity for my first return finally came in 1976 on the occasion of my parents' 40th wedding anniversary, a milestone celebration that I simply could not miss. This golden anniversary represented not just their enduring love for each other but also their resilience through the war years, the German occupation, and the challenging period of rebuilding that followed. My siblings and I had been planning this celebration for months, and despite the financial sacrifice it represented, I knew I had to be there to honor my parents and their journey together.

I decided to take my oldest daughter with me on this momentous trip, partly because she was old enough, at 15, to appreciate the significance of meeting her Dutch grandparents and extended family, and partly because I wanted her to understand her heritage and see the country where her father had grown up. She was mature enough to handle the long journey and curious enough about her roots to make the most of the experience. My wife couldn't make the trip because she was taking care of the rest of our family and the younger children back home.

With five other children still at home, including some relatively young, Martha's presence was absolutely essential for maintaining our household and ensuring the flower business continued to operate smoothly in my absence.

This first return to Holland after so many years was deeply emotional. Walking through the streets of my childhood, seeing how much had changed yet how much remained the same, and reuniting with family members who had aged significantly in my absence created a bittersweet mixture of joy and melancholy. My daughter served as a bridge between my past and present, watching with wide eyes as I pointed out landmarks from my youth and listening intently as relatives shared stories about our family history. The anniversary celebration itself was a beautiful testament to love and perseverance, bringing together family members who had scattered across different continents but remained connected by bonds that neither time nor distance could break.

Cinema and Family Connections

My daughter and I arrived in Holland as the only people in our travel group who spoke English, since my daughter doesn't speak Dutch, and we were navigating this foreign country together. By an extraordinary stroke of timing, we happened to arrive just as the film "A Bridge Too Far" was being filmed in the area. This epic war movie depicted Operation Market Garden, the ambitious but ultimately failed Allied operation that took place in Arnhem in September 1944. The filmmakers had chosen to shoot in Deventer rather than the actual Arnhem location because Deventer still had a bridge and surrounding architecture that closely resembled how Arnhem had looked during the war years. Modern Arnhem had been rebuilt and no longer retained the 1940s appearance that the movie required, but Deventer had maintained much of its wartime character, making it the perfect cinematic substitute. The irony wasn't lost on me that this recreation was taking place only four miles away from where I had actually lived during those tumultuous war years.

The production attracted a remarkable influx of veterans from England and other Allied countries to serve as advisors and extras for the movie. The film crew had transported authentic period equipment from England, including restored jeeps, military vehicles, uniforms, and weapons, all of which accurately reflected the World War II era. Since this was a British production with significant financial backing, many British actors, crew members, and military consultants flooded into our small Dutch town, transforming the quiet streets into a bustling international film set. The situation became quite amusing when some locals began assuming that my daughter and I were part of the film crew, simply because we were the only ones speaking English in casual conversation. Our American accents and obvious familiarity with the language made us stand out among the Dutch locals, leading to several mistaken identity moments that we found both flattering and entertaining.

I still treasure the photographs I took during filming, capturing both the behind-the-scenes action and the carefully choreographed battle sequences. These images hold special significance because I witnessed firsthand the historical events being recreated on screen. Having lived through Operation Market Garden as a young person in 1944, I could appreciate the filmmakers' attention to detail in recreating those harrowing days. Watching actors portray events I had experienced decades earlier created a surreal connection between past and present, making the entire experience both nostalgic and emotionally powerful.

Five years later, I was finally able to fulfill a long-held dream of taking two of my daughters to Holland to visit my remaining family members. This trip allowed me to show them the places where I had grown up, from the house where I was born to the schools I had attended before the war disrupted everything. We walked through the neighborhoods where I had played as a child, visited the church where my family had worshipped, and met relatives who still remembered stories about our family's wartime experiences. The girls were fascinated to see the physical locations that had shaped their father's early life, and I enjoyed watching their reactions as they began to understand the journey that had eventually brought our family to America.

The logistics and expense of taking the entire family to Europe meant that these trips had to be spread out over many years. It took us a couple more years of saving and planning before I was finally able to take my wife and my youngest daughter to Holland for their first visit. Martha had heard countless stories about my homeland over the years, but seeing it through her own eyes gave her a deeper understanding of my background and the experiences that had shaped my worldview. Our youngest daughter, being closer in age to the one I was when I left Holland, seemed particularly moved by visiting the places where her father had lived through such dramatic historical events.

In 1992, I arranged a special father-son trip, taking just my oldest son to Holland and then touring other parts of Europe together. This one-on-one time allowed us to have deeper conversations about family history and gave him the opportunity to ask questions about the war years and my decision to immigrate to America. We spent hours walking through Dutch museums, visiting historical sites, and talking with older relatives who could share their own memories of our family's past. Initially, I had planned to take both of my sons on this trip, but my youngest son had decided to get married that year, and the timing of his wedding preparations made it impossible for him to join us. The wedding took precedence, naturally, but it meant that his European adventure would have to wait.

It took another full decade before I was finally able to take my youngest son to Europe in 2002, but the wait proved worthwhile. By then, he was older and perhaps more appreciative of the historical significance of what he was seeing. This final family pilgrimage completed my goal of ensuring that all of my children had the opportunity to understand their Dutch heritage and see the places where their family story began, creating a bridge between the old world and the new that would be passed down to future generations.

CHAPTER 15

A Life of Service

Men's Club and Knights of Columbus

* * *

When we first settled in Half Moon Bay, we became members of the Our Lady of the Pilar Parish, which became our spiritual home for many years. Looking to deepen my faith and connect with other Catholic men in the community, I joined the Men's Club, an organization that provides valuable opportunities for Catholic men to grow in their faith through regular prayer groups, in-depth Bible study sessions, weekend retreats, and meaningful discussions about how to live out Catholic values in our daily lives. These gatherings became an important source of both spiritual nourishment and male fellowship during the demanding years of building our flower business.

In 1980, a new Knights of Columbus Council was started in Half Moon Bay, and I was one of the chartered members. I was, however, not very active during my first years of membership because the demanding work schedule on our flower farm often conflicted with their regular meeting times. The early-morning starts and long days required by our agricultural business meant I was not always able to attend the evening meetings and social events that were central to the organization's community-building efforts. Despite my limited availability for regular meetings, I became very active in our Council's biggest annual fundraiser during Half Moon Bay's famous pumpkin festival each October. The week-long community celebration drew thousands of visitors to our coastal town, and the Knights of Columbus played a crucial role in the festivities.

Our preparation for the pumpkin festival was intensive and required tremendous coordination among all the members. We spent an entire week before the festival meticulously preparing hundreds of pounds of fresh artichokes to sell throughout the festival weekend and raise funds for our various charitable causes. The work involved cleaning, trimming, and cooking the artichokes in large batches, then packaging them for sale to hungry festival-goers. The aroma of steaming artichokes filled our preparation area, and the camaraderie among the volunteers made even the most tedious tasks enjoyable. These fundraising efforts supported local charities, scholarships for Catholic school students, and various community service projects throughout the year.

When we eventually moved to Templeton for our retirement years, we discovered there was no Catholic parish directly in town, so we joined the parish in Atascadero, about five miles from our new home. This turned out to be a fortunate circumstance, as Atascadero had an exceptionally active parish community in which the Knights of Columbus had already established a strong and influential presence. Since I was no longer working the demanding hours required by farming, I finally had the time and energy to become one of the organization's most active and dedicated members. This increased involvement allowed me to participate fully in their charitable works, attend regular meetings, and take on leadership roles that had been impossible during my working years. I served two years as Grand Knight of Santa Lucia Council in Atascadero.

Membership of the Kiwanis Club

It was also during our time in Templeton that I joined the local Kiwanis Club, becoming part of a well-known global network of volunteers dedicated to improving the world one child and one community at a time. Founded in 1915 with the motto "Serving the Children of the World," Kiwanis clubs focus on serving children and communities through ambitious service projects and coordinated fundraising activities. Our local club members typically met weekly to plan and coordinate community service initiatives, discuss ways to support local causes and organizations, and work collaboratively on projects specifically designed to benefit youth development, educational opportunities, and overall community welfare. I remained an active and committed member of the Kiwanis Club for about 14 years, participating in everything from scholarship programs to community cleanup projects.

Big Brothers, Big Sisters

Perhaps most personally rewarding was my involvement with Big Brothers Big Sisters, one of the United States' oldest and largest youth mentoring organizations. Founded in 1904 with over a century of experience in youth development, this organization serves hundreds of thousands of children annually through a network of local affiliates established across the entire country. The program's fundamental approach involves pairing carefully screened adult volunteers, known as "Bigs," with children and teens, known as "Littles," to create meaningful relationships that provide positive role models and consistent emotional support during crucial developmental years.

Our mission focused on helping young people reach their full potential through professionally supported, one-to-one mentoring relationships that often lasted for years. As "Bigs," we committed to spending regular, quality time with our assigned "Littles," engaging in activities that ranged from playing sports and attending movies to simply hanging out and talking about life's challenges and opportunities. These relationships often became deeply meaningful to both the mentor and the child, creating bonds that extended far beyond the formal program requirements. Through my years with Big Brothers Big Sisters, I had the privilege of watching several young people grow into confident, successful adults, knowing that our time together had played a small but important role in their development and future success.

Through Big Brothers Big Sisters, I sponsored one particular child who has remained close to my heart—a nine-year-old boy from a single-parent household whose mother was struggling to provide both emotional support and financial stability. This young man needed not just academic help, but someone to believe in him and show him possibilities beyond his immediate circumstances. I would take him out to lunch at local restaurants where we could talk without distractions, and to various after-school activities like baseball games, visits to the library, and sometimes just walks through the park where he could share what was happening in his life. Over the months and years of our relationship, it was a genuine delight to watch him gradually build self-confidence, develop crucial social skills through our interactions and group activities, and steadily improve his academic performance as he began to see education as a pathway to a better future. The transformation wasn't immediate, but seeing him grow from a shy, uncertain child into a confident young person who believed in his own potential made every hour we spent together worthwhile.

Habitat for Humanity

With considerably more time on my hands than when I was working the demanding schedule of our flower farm, I decided to expand my volunteer work and make an even greater impact in my community. That decision led me to join Habitat for Humanity, a nonprofit organization founded in 1976 with a mission to help families build and improve places to call home. This organization operates on the principle that everyone deserves a decent, affordable place to live, regardless of their economic circumstances. We worked to construct quality, affordable housing for low-income families who otherwise couldn't afford homeownership due to rising real estate costs and limited access to traditional financing. The program's unique approach requires families to contribute "sweat equity" by working alongside volunteers to build not only their own homes but also those of other families in the program, fostering a sense of community ownership and mutual support.

During my years with Habitat for Humanity, we constructed three complete homes in Paso Robles in San Luis Obispo County, building each house from the foundation up through final inspection. The process typically took several months per home, with volunteers working weekends and the recipient families contributing hundreds of hours of labor. It was genuinely a delight to work alongside the families whose homes we were building, sharing meals during lunch breaks, celebrating small milestones like completing the framing or installing the roof, and witnessing their excitement as their dream of homeownership gradually became reality. These weren't just construction projects; they were life-changing experiences for families living in substandard housing or struggling to afford unaffordable rent.

Martha's arrival in the United States in 1956

My friend, Peter Van Os, acting as the best man at my wedding on November 26, 1960

On our wedding day as we emerged from the Church. One of the few pictures taken that day.

Our young family in Half Moon Bay

Our family in Half Moon Bay in 1978

Our children in 1979

Me in army uniform in 1958

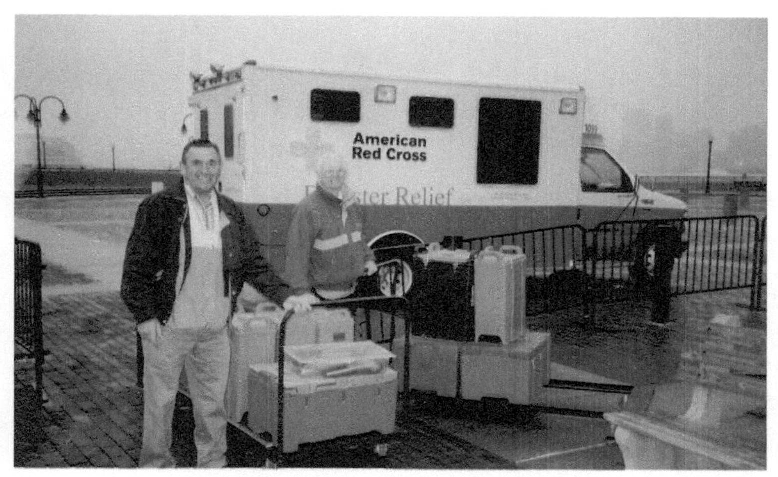

Me as an American Red Cross Volunteer

Me irrigating a farm in Gustine, California, July 1959

Our greenhouses under construction in Half Moon Bay, California

A greenhouse under construction in Pescadero, California

1995 Farmer of the Year Award: One of two awards I received.

Our nursery in Pescadero, California

CHAPTER 16

Disaster Relief

* * *

A few years later, seeking to expand my community service into emergency response, I also joined the American Red Cross, an organization that provides critical assistance during disasters and emergencies. We trained extensively in disaster-relief protocols and maintained readiness to respond to local disasters, including house fires, floods, earthquakes, and other emergencies that could displace families and disrupt communities. I remember being called out at two o'clock in the morning to respond to a devastating mobile home park fire that had spread rapidly through the dry California landscape. The scene was chaotic and heartbreaking, with people scampering everywhere in various stages of undress—many of them in their pajamas and nightgowns, having barely escaped with their lives as the flames consumed their homes. Entire mobile homes had been burned to ashes within minutes, leaving families with nothing but the clothes on their backs and traumatic memories of their narrow escape.

Our immediate mission was to ensure everyone's safety by getting displaced residents to secure locations away from the smoke and continuing danger, then addressing their most basic needs. We made emergency trips to Walmart and other stores to purchase essential clothing items to keep people warm during the cool night hours, arranged temporary accommodations in local motels until more permanent housing solutions could be found, and provided emotional support to families who had lost everything they owned. These local emergency responses taught me valuable lessons about human resilience in the face of sudden tragedy and the importance of having trained volunteers ready to respond immediately when disaster strikes.

The Red Cross also deployed me to much larger disaster zones that required coordinated responses from multiple states. I was sent to North Carolina as part of a specialized team helping victims of a major hurricane that had struck the coastal and inland areas with devastating force. The scale of destruction was absolutely overwhelming—entire neighborhoods had been flattened by winds and flooding, families had been separated during evacuation efforts, and the infrastructure damage made normal relief efforts extremely challenging. Working in that environment required not just physical stamina but emotional resilience, as we encountered heartbreaking stories of loss while maintaining hope and providing practical assistance to help communities begin the long process of rebuilding.

I also recall spending three intensive weeks in San Bernardino County in Southern California. A massive wildfire had spread across thousands of acres and was threatening numerous communities. The fire caused significant property damage and required the evacuation of entire neighborhoods as unpredictable winds pushed the flames in multiple directions. Our role involved not just firefighting support but also managing evacuation centers, reuniting families separated amid the chaos, and providing essential services to displaced residents unsure whether their homes would still be standing when they were allowed to return.

Ground Zero Experience

Then came September 11, 2001, when terrorists attacked and destroyed the Twin Towers in New York City, creating one of the most devastating disasters in American history. I was deployed to Ground Zero for one whole month, working alongside thousands of firefighters, police officers, construction workers, and other Red Cross personnel in the massive rescue and recovery efforts. The experience was unlike anything I had ever encountered—the scale of destruction, the emotional weight of the tragedy, and the incredible dedication of everyone working around the clock to find survivors and eventually to recover victims created an atmosphere that was simultaneously heartbreaking and inspiring.

Working at Ground Zero meant twelve-hour shifts in dangerous conditions, breathing air filled with dust and debris, climbing over twisted metal and concrete rubble, and maintaining hope even when the chances of finding survivors grew increasingly slim. We provided food, water, and emotional support to the professional rescue workers pushing themselves beyond normal human limits, and we helped coordinate the massive logistical effort required to manage this unprecedented disaster response. What an experience that was—one that lives with you for your entire life, changing your perspective on human fragility, resilience, and the profound importance of people coming together during humanity's darkest moments.

My African Mission

My volunteer work eventually took me to Africa, specifically Uganda, fulfilling a dream planted in my heart decades earlier. I was a member of a medical mission group called "His Healing Hands," which operated as a specialized international service. This dedicated team of medical professionals and support volunteers traveled annually to countries where medical services were in dire need, bringing essential healthcare to underserved populations who had little or no access to modern medical care. The commitment required significant personal investment, both financially and emotionally, but the opportunity to make a direct impact on people's lives made every sacrifice worthwhile.

I believe my attraction to volunteer work and international service was born when I was still a young person in Holland during the 1940s and early 1950s. In those post-war years, I frequently saw missionaries leaving Holland to embark on dedicated missionary work in Africa, Indonesia, and other parts of the developing world where Dutch Protestant and Catholic churches had established missions. These departures were significant community events that captured the imagination of young people like myself who were seeking purpose and adventure beyond our small Dutch towns. The missionaries often organized elaborate fundraising fairs and community gatherings where people would come together to hear them share compelling stories about their work abroad, describing both the challenges and rewards of serving in distant lands.

During these events, the missionaries would not only raise funds for their ongoing work but also actively canvas and recruit young people of our age to consider joining them as missionaries, presenting service work as both a calling and an adventure. The stories they told were vivid and inspiring—tales of building schools and medical clinics, bringing education to children who had never held a book, and providing healthcare to communities that had been forgotten by the modern world. From what they told us about their experiences, I became deeply interested in the possibility of going for missionary work in the Belgian Congo, a vast territory in Central Africa where conditions were reportedly among the most challenging and the need for assistance was greatest. I was still very young at that time, just about 12 years old, but the seed of international service had been firmly planted in my mind and heart.

It would take several decades before my childhood dream of visiting Africa finally came true when I joined "His Healing Hands" medical mission to Uganda. The trip was quite expensive, since participants were expected to largely finance their own travel, accommodations, and living expenses during the mission, but the experience proved worth every penny. The comprehensive medical team I was privileged to work with visited remote villages that had rarely been seen by any organized medical team, bringing modern healthcare to people living hours or even days away from the nearest clinic or hospital.

Even though there were dedicated Protestant missionaries already working in that region of Uganda, providing spiritual guidance and some basic community services, they weren't always medically equipped or trained to handle the complex medical needs of the local population. "His Healing Hands" had the wisdom to contact these established missionaries a full year ahead of our planned visit, giving them time to coordinate with local leaders and prepare the communities for our arrival. The resident missionaries, with their extensive on-the-ground contacts and deep understanding of local customs and languages, facilitated our work in ways our team would have been unable to accomplish independently. They notified the people in surrounding areas of our upcoming arrival, spreading word through traditional communication networks that reached even the most isolated communities.

It was absolutely amazing to witness how many people would travel significant distances to our makeshift clinics for free medical consultations, many of them walking for hours, carrying sick children or supporting elderly family members who hadn't seen a doctor in years, or perhaps ever. We brought substantial quantities of essential medicines and vitamins, donated free of charge by pharmaceutical companies and medical supply organizations in the United States, allowing us to treat conditions ranging from basic infections to more serious chronic illnesses. It was genuinely a delight to see how deeply appreciative the population was of our work among them, with grateful patients often offering small gifts of food or handmade items despite their own poverty.

The week after our first village clinic, we packed up our medical supplies and traveled to another small village about 150 miles away, over challenging roads, little more than dirt paths carved through the African bush. These were truly remote villages, situated far from any urban areas or infrastructure, where the inhabitants had never received any form of organized medical care throughout their lives. Not only did we offer them free medical consultations and distribute essential medicines, but we also spent considerable time providing health education, offering practical advice on nutrition, sanitation, disease prevention, and basic first aid to help them stay healthier between our visits.

Our medical team consisted of three dedicated doctors with various specialties and several experienced nurses, and it was inspiring to watch them work with absolute dedication and professionalism under far-from-ideal circumstances. We operated in simple buildings with basic electricity, limited clean water, and minimal medical equipment beyond what we had transported ourselves. Yet these medical professionals adapted to the conditions with remarkable grace and effectiveness, treating patients with the same care and attention they would provide in modern American hospitals. All of us were volunteers who had taken time away from our regular jobs and families to participate in this mission, united by a shared commitment to service and human compassion.

Uganda proved to be a breathtakingly beautiful country, with rolling green hills, diverse wildlife, and warm, welcoming people who embodied resilience despite significant economic challenges. We were fortunate that there was no armed conflict or political instability in the region during our time there, allowing us to work safely and focus entirely on our medical mission without concerns about security or evacuation. The natural beauty of the landscape, combined with the profound human connections we made, created memories that have remained vivid and meaningful throughout all the years since that transformative experience.

CHAPTER 17

Health Challenges and Family Support

* * *

In 2012, our peaceful retirement life was suddenly disrupted when I received devastating news: I was diagnosed with lymphoma, a severe form of cancer that would require immediate and aggressive treatment. The diagnosis came as a shock, as I had been feeling relatively healthy and active for my age. But there was no time for denial or delay—my doctors recommended that I begin intensive chemotherapy treatment right away to give me the best possible chance of defeating the disease.

The chemotherapy regimen was grueling and exhausting, involving multiple rounds of powerful drugs designed to destroy the cancer cells throughout my body. The side effects were significant—nausea, fatigue, hair loss, and a general feeling of weakness that made even simple daily tasks challenging. However, by God's grace and the skill of my medical team, the treatment proved to be successful. The aggressive approach worked, and the lymphoma was eliminated from my system, giving me a clean bill of health and a new lease on life.

While I was profoundly grateful for my recovery and the opportunity to continue living, the cancer treatment had taken a considerable toll on my physical strength and energy levels. I found that I could no longer handle the physical demands of working on the acre of land I had been tending in Templeton. The planting, weeding, pruning, and general maintenance that I had once enjoyed as relaxing retirement activities now seemed overwhelming and exhausting. My body simply wasn't capable of the sustained physical effort required to properly care for the trees and flower gardens I had lovingly cultivated over the years.

Martha and I began realizing that our living situation needed to change to accommodate my altered health status and our increased need for family support. We decided to move closer to our daughter, Alice, and her family in Gilroy, California, where she could provide more regular assistance, and where we could be more involved in our grandchildren's daily lives.

After careful consideration and family discussions, we decided to sell our house in Templeton, where we had enjoyed many happy retirement years and built meaningful community connections. The process of downsizing and leaving a place where we had established roots was emotionally challenging, but the prospect of being closer to family during this vulnerable time in our lives made the transition feel like the right choice.

New Beginnings in Gilroy: Faith and Family

The move to Gilroy proved to be one of the best decisions we could have made. We found a comfortable home that suited our needs perfectly, and more importantly, we now live only 15 minutes away from our daughter and her family. This proximity has been invaluable, allowing for regular visits, shared family meals, and the kind of spontaneous interactions that make family relationships thrive. Our daughter can easily check on us when needed, help with medical appointments or household tasks, and include us in family activities without the burden of long-distance travel. For us, being close to our grandchildren during their formative years has been an unexpected gift that emerged from a difficult health crisis, proving that sometimes life's challenges can lead to new opportunities for connection and joy.

One of the first things I did when we settled in Gilroy was to join the local Knights of Columbus council, seeking to continue the faith-based community service that had been such an important part of my life in Templeton. Drawing on my decades of experience with the organization, I volunteered to serve as the recruiting officer, a role that enabled me to draw on my understanding of the Knights' mission and values to attract new members to our growing council. Over the years in this position, I have successfully recruited many of the current officers and active members of our Knights of Columbus Council in Gilroy, helping to build a strong foundation of dedicated Catholic men committed to charity, unity, fraternity, and patriotism. This recruitment work has been particularly satisfying because it allows me to share the same sense of purpose and community that the Knights provided for me during my earlier years, while building relationships with younger men who are just beginning their own journeys of faith and service.

Our Eight Grandchildren: A Source of Pride and Joy

We have been blessed with eight wonderful grandchildren, each unique in their talents and aspirations, and all of whom have attended high school and pursued higher education. Watching them grow from curious children into accomplished young adults has been one of the greatest joys of our later years. All have already graduated from college with degrees in various fields. Some are also pursuing higher educational goals with determination and focus. It is always such a tremendous privilege and source of pride for Martha and me to attend their graduation ceremonies, regardless of where those celebrations take place across the country.

These graduation trips have taken us to many different states, creating travel adventures that we never anticipated during our working years. We have celebrated graduations from California to Massachusetts, as well as in Washington, Idaho, Oklahoma, and South Carolina. Each ceremony represents not just individual achievement but also the fulfillment of the educational dreams that Martha and I held for our entire family when we first made a financial sacrifice to ensure our children could attend college.

For many years, we maintained the wonderful tradition of hosting large family gatherings at our home for special events, holidays, and celebrations. These occasions would bring together all the kids and grandchildren—around 18 people in total—filling the house with laughter, storytelling, and the kind of multi-generational bonding that strengthens family ties over the years. It was such a genuine delight to have them all with us, watching the grandchildren play together, listening to our adult children share parenting experiences, and creating memories that we knew would last long after we were gone.

However, as our grandchildren have grown older and pursued their educational and career opportunities, getting the entire extended family together has become increasingly challenging. For some years now, the grandchildren have been scattered across the country for their studies and early careers, making it difficult to coordinate schedules to gather everyone in one place. While we miss those large family celebrations, we understand and support their pursuits of education and opportunity, knowing that the foundation of family love and connection we built during their younger years will sustain our relationships regardless of geographical distance.

CHAPTER 18

Keeping in Touch with the Netherlands

* * *

On the personal side, I am the oldest of seven siblings. After living in the United States for 10 years, I helped one of my sisters immigrate here. She now lives in Desert Hot Springs, California. The rest of my family—two brothers and three sisters—remain in the Netherlands. As we all grow older, we've come to realize the importance of reconnecting in person, so I make it a point to visit them every few years, although international travel can be pretty expensive.

Growing up as the eldest child during a time of significant hardship had a lasting impact on me. Our family endured many difficulties in the aftermath of the war, which affected individuals and the nation as a whole. In those days, higher education was not something most people even considered. As a result, I left school at 15 and began working full-time on a farm. I've been working ever since. That early start instilled in me a strong work ethic and a deep sense of responsibility—values that have shaped much of my life.

Our children, understandably, never learned to speak Dutch. Since Dutch isn't commonly spoken in California and there were few opportunities for them to practice or learn from native speakers, it simply wasn't practical. However, they did learn some Spanish, their mother's native tongue, which proved much more useful given California's large Spanish-speaking population. This linguistic choice reflected the practical realities of our new home while still maintaining a connection to Martha's cultural roots.

I grew up in Holland during a time when it was completely and uniquely Dutch—a period that feels almost unimaginable today. This was long before the introduction of the euro, before European borders were opened, and decades before the formation of the European Union transformed the continent. Everything about European travel and culture was fundamentally different then. The continent was a patchwork of distinct nations, each fiercely protective of its sovereignty and cultural identity.

Interestingly, it was during the 1960s that many things began to change dramatically in Holland, with American culture gaining unprecedented prominence throughout the country. American music filled the radio waves, Hollywood films dominated movie theaters, and the English language became increasingly important in Dutch society. This cultural shift created a generational divide within my own family back in the Netherlands. My two eldest brothers never learned to speak English because they simply never had the opportunity or pressing need during their formative years. However, my four sisters and their children all became proficient in English as the language became more essential in Dutch society.

The transformation has been so complete that if you were to visit Holland today and speak only English, you might not even realize that Dutch is the native language. Nearly everyone you encounter—from shopkeepers to taxi drivers to government officials—can communicate fluently in English. This phenomenon extends far beyond the Netherlands; it seems to be the case throughout much of Europe, where English has become the universal second language, bridging cultural and national boundaries in ways that would have been unimaginable when Martha and I first arrived in America as young immigrants seeking our fortune in a new land.

Even as late as 1976, when I made my first return trip to Holland after immigrating to America, the reality of European travel was cumbersome and bureaucratic. As we journeyed through Belgium, Luxembourg, and Germany, we encountered border crossings at every national boundary, where officials scrutinized our passports and stamped them with official entry marks. Each country had its own currency, requiring us to exchange money at every border—Belgian francs to Luxembourg francs to German deutschmarks—with exchange rates and fees eating into our travel budget. The process was time-consuming and reminded us constantly that we were moving between sovereign nations with their own laws, customs, and monetary systems.

CHAPTER 19

Visiting Alaska

A Brother's Dream Fulfilled

* * *

My younger brother Jan had harbored a lifelong dream that seemed as distant as the northern lights themselves—visiting Alaska. For as long as I could remember, he spoke of it with the kind of wistful longing that comes from dreams deferred. When I finally retired in 1998, I knew exactly how I wanted to mark this new chapter of my life: by making Jan's dream come true.

The invitation I extended to him sparked an excitement I hadn't seen in years. Without the means to fly, we embraced the adventurous alternative—a cross-country odyssey in my pickup truck, armed with nothing more than a small tent and an unshakeable determination to reach the Last Frontier together.

Our journey began with a meaningful detour to Nevada, where we spent precious days with my son, Albert, before pointing our compass northward. The route that unfolded before us was nothing short of epic: through the diverse landscapes of Oregon and Washington, across the Canadian border into British Columbia, then through the vast wilderness of Yukon Territory, finally arriving in Alaska—a staggering 4,000 miles from our starting point.

What began as a six-week adventure became something far more profound. We spent 40 nights under canvas, our small tent becoming a nightly sanctuary where two brothers, separated by over four decades of silence, slowly rediscovered each other. In Fairbanks, we camped beneath skies that seemed to stretch into infinity, each evening bringing us closer not just to our destination, but to each other.

The Alaska Marine Highway provided one of our most memorable interludes—the ferry journey from Haines to Bellingham, Washington, offered breathtaking views of pristine coastline and towering glaciers. By journey's end, we had covered over 9,000 miles, but the true distance we traveled was measured in rekindled brotherhood.

One moment remains etched in my memory. Our planned route through Yosemite to Nevada, where my son Albert lived, was blocked when Tioga Pass remained closed for winter. Redirected and somewhat disappointed, we found ourselves camping on snow-covered hills. I awoke that morning to a sight so spectacular it defied description—a pristine blanket of snow transforming the entire landscape into a winter wonderland. Jan, coming from Holland, where snow rarely graces the ground, stood transfixed by the ethereal beauty surrounding us. His wonder was infectious, and in that moment, I realized that sometimes the most beautiful destinations are the unplanned ones.

From there, we took the Sonora Pass route into Nevada, but that snowy morning had already given us something more valuable than any planned destination could offer.

For Jan, this wasn't just a trip—it was the fulfillment of a lifelong dream. Years later, even on his deathbed, he spoke of our Alaskan adventure with the same excitement that had lit up his face when I first proposed it. Those six weeks had become the golden thread that rewove the fabric of our brotherhood, transforming forty years of silence into a treasure trove of shared memories that would comfort him in his final moments.

The greatest gift wasn't the breathtaking vistas of Alaska or the majesty of snow-covered mountains—it was the rediscovery of my brother and the knowledge that together, we had turned a dream into the adventure of a lifetime.

CHAPTER 20

Respect For the Fallen

* * *

During each visit I made to Holland with my children, I made it a point to take them to the American Cemetery in Margraten, a small village near Maastricht, located in the southern part of the Netherlands. This vast and solemn cemetery serves as a powerful testament to the enormous sacrifice made by American soldiers who died during the brutal campaign to liberate Europe from Nazi occupation. I felt my American-born children needed to understand and witness firsthand the price paid for the freedom we all enjoyed. The rows upon rows of white crosses and Stars of David stretching across the manicured grounds provided a visceral reminder of the cost of liberty.

The most memorable visit occurred in 2012, when my youngest son accompanied me. By pure coincidence, we arrived on Memorial Day, though we reached the cemetery too late to participate in the formal ceremony, which had taken place earlier that morning. Despite missing the official proceedings, we were greeted by a breathtaking sight: hundreds of floral wreaths and bouquets had been carefully placed throughout the cemetery grounds, creating a colorful tapestry of remembrance. These tributes had been sent by organizations from around the world, each one representing communities that still remembered and honored the sacrifice of these fallen soldiers.

I salute the memory of Morris Tracy!

While living in Templeton, I was a member of the California Rare Fruit Growers Central Coast Chapter. We had field trips on one Saturday per month. One cold Saturday morning, I saw a member of our group wearing a distinctive jacket emblazoned with the emblem of Apeldoorn, a town located just a few miles from my childhood home. His name was Morris Tracy, and as we began talking, I learned his remarkable story.

He explained that he had been a Canadian soldier during World War II and had participated in the liberation of that exact region of Holland where I had grown up. After the war ended, he returned to Canada, where he built a career working for an electric company. Years later, like so many others, he decided to seek new opportunities and migrated to California, where he found employment with Pacific Gas & Electric Company (PG&E) in the Central Valley. After his retirement, he had settled in the peaceful coastal town of Arroyo Grande.

As we continued our conversation about the war and its aftermath, I discovered something that left me absolutely astounded: Morris had been one of the actual soldiers who had liberated my hometown. The coincidence seemed almost impossible—here I was, thousands of miles from home, meeting a man who had literally helped free the very streets where I had played as a child. The emotional impact of this realization was overwhelming.

Our chance meeting came 59 years after the war and blossomed into a meaningful friendship. We arranged to visit each other's homes, and Morris came to my house bearing precious mementos from that historic operation—detailed military maps, photographs from the liberation campaign, and meticulously kept records documenting the day-by-day progress of the Allied advance through our region of Holland. His unit had marched down my childhood street during the liberation, and tragically, their commanding officer had been killed in action right there in my neighborhood. A commemorative plaque had been installed at that very spot to honor the fallen commander's sacrifice.

Morris explained that he had made this trip to Holland as part of a veterans' reunion that occurred every ten years, bringing together surviving soldiers who had fought in that campaign. These gatherings served not only as opportunities for old comrades to reconnect, but also as solemn occasions to honor their fallen brothers and to ensure that the younger generations in both Canada and Holland would never forget the price of their freedom. Meeting Morris that day created a profound personal connection to the larger historical events that had shaped both our lives and our countries.

For the 60th anniversary of Holland's liberation in 2005, the Dutch government extended a special invitation to all surviving Canadian veterans, including Morris, to return to our town for what would likely be their final official commemoration. The entire community came together to organize a grand parade in their honor, with thousands of residents lining the streets to cheer these aging heroes. Local dignitaries and government officials delivered heartfelt speeches expressing our nation's enduring gratitude for the tremendous sacrifices these brave men had made six decades earlier to free us from German occupation. The celebration was both joyous and bittersweet, as everyone understood this would probably be the last time such a gathering would be possible.

Since that memorable 2005 anniversary, no similar large-scale celebrations have been organized, for the simple and sobering reason that most of those courageous veterans have passed away. The few who remain alive are now in their nineties, and many are too frail to make the transatlantic journey. Time has claimed nearly all of those young soldiers who once marched through our streets as liberators, leaving behind only memories, photographs, and the grateful hearts of those they saved.

During one of our conversations, I told Morris about my brothers and sisters who still lived in Holland and invited him to visit them on his next trip to the Netherlands. To my delight, he accepted the invitation and made the effort to meet my family during his subsequent visit. The encounter was deeply meaningful for my siblings, who were able to personally thank one of the soldiers who had helped secure their freedom. Later, when my brothers and sisters visited me in California, we arranged a reciprocal visit to Morris's home in Arroyo Grande. These exchanges strengthened the bond between our families and created lasting connections that transcended nationality and generation.

For ten years, Morris and I maintained a close friendship, regularly corresponding and visiting whenever possible. He was truly an extraordinary man—someone who had experienced history firsthand and carried those experiences with grace, humility, and wisdom. The mathematics of our friendship never ceased to amaze me: he had been just twenty-one years old when he fought as a soldier in the campaign to liberate my country, while I was only eight years old, probably playing in the very streets his unit was securing. The fact that after fifty-nine years had passed, we would meet again by pure chance in California, specifically in San Luis Obispo County, seemed like something orchestrated by fate itself. Morris lived to the age of ninety-five before peacefully passing away, leaving me with countless fond memories of our friendship and the stories he shared about those pivotal days in world history.

It has now been over eighty years since World War II ended, yet the importance of remembering and teaching these lessons has not diminished. In fact, it has become more crucial than ever. We must continue to educate our children and grandchildren about the vital role that Allied troops—American, Canadian, British, and others—played in liberating Europe from Nazi tyranny. Even though today's young people have no personal connection to the war and often know very little about its significance, it remains our solemn responsibility as the older generation to share these stories with them. We must help them understand that the freedoms they enjoy today were not freely given but were purchased with the blood and sacrifice of countless brave men and women.

CHAPTER 21

I Salute All Veterans!

* * *

My years of service working for the National Guard provided me with valuable insights into military service and deepened my appreciation for those who serve our country. Today, I am proud to be an active member of the American Legion, and I make a point of participating in all its activities and commemorative events. Whether it's Veterans Day in November or Memorial Day in May, I attend these solemn ceremonies to honor those who served and those who made the ultimate sacrifice. More importantly, I make sure to bring my grandchildren to these events, using them as teaching opportunities to instill in them a deep respect for our flag, our soldiers, and our veterans.

I tell my grandchildren that without the courage and sacrifice of American soldiers—along with their Allied counterparts—we would not enjoy the freedoms that we sometimes thoughtlessly take for granted in our daily lives. These young people have grown up in an era of unprecedented liberty and prosperity, making it difficult for them to imagine a world without such freedoms. Through these ceremonies and the stories I share, I hope to ensure that they understand the precious nature of liberty and the ongoing responsibility we all have to protect and preserve it for future generations.

As an immigrant to this country, I hold a profound appreciation for all that America has given me—an appreciation that perhaps runs deeper than it does for many Americans who were born and raised here. Having experienced life under a different system and having made the conscious choice to build my life in this nation, I understand intimately the precious nature of American freedoms. Too many young people today seem to take everything for granted—the ability to speak freely, to worship as they choose, to pursue their dreams without government interference, to vote for their leaders, and to live without fear of oppression. These rights, which they view as natural and automatic, are rare and fragile gifts that have been hard-won through centuries of struggle and sacrifice.

I know firsthand what it takes to achieve and maintain the freedom we now enjoy, having witnessed both the devastation of war and the painstaking process of rebuilding that follows. Such freedoms are not self-sustaining; they must be actively maintained and defended by each generation. It is our army and the dedicated men and women who serve in all branches of the armed forces who stand as guardians of these liberties, ensuring that our way of life remains protected from those who would seek to destroy or undermine it.

I am deeply happy and proud to have been part of this great endeavor, even in what I consider a relatively small way. While I never served in combat zones or participated in major battles,

I was honored to serve in the United States Army. That service, however brief or limited in scope, connected me to a long tradition of Americans who have answered their country's call. The pride I feel in that service has only grown stronger over the years, as I've come to better understand the vital role military service plays in preserving our democratic institutions.

Whenever my grandchildren came to visit during patriotic holidays—the Fourth of July, Memorial Day, or Veterans Day—I would make it a priority to take them to local parades and ceremonies. Those events provided powerful visual lessons about why it was so important to respect and honor the men and women who have fought, and continue to fight, for our country. I wanted them to see the aging veterans marching with pride despite their physical limitations, to witness the solemn ceremonies at war memorials, and to understand that real people—neighbors, family members, ordinary Americans—who have willingly put themselves in harm's way to preserve the freedoms my grandchildren have enjoyed every single day.

I am genuinely glad to see that veterans are receiving more respect and recognition than ever before. The American public is beginning to realize and truly appreciate the enormous sacrifices that service members have made on our behalf. There's a growing understanding that these men and women have given up years of their lives, time with their families, and in many cases, their physical and mental health, all in service to something larger than themselves.

Every war brings tragedy and sorrow, but the Vietnam War stands out as particularly heartbreaking, not just because of the combat itself, but because of how our society treated the soldiers when they returned home. It was deeply shameful to witness how those brave young men, who had answered their country's call and served with honor in an unpopular conflict, were met with hostility, protests, and even hatred when they came back to American soil. Many were spat upon, called names, and made to feel ashamed of their service. That treatment was a dark chapter in our nation's history, and I'm thankful to see that things have changed dramatically for the better since then.

Today's returning veterans are greeted with ceremonies, parades, and genuine expressions of gratitude from their communities. However, we still have important work to do in teaching our children and grandchildren what it truly means to serve in our country's armed forces. We must help them understand that military service involves real sacrifice—separation from loved ones, physical danger, and the willingness to put the needs of the nation above personal comfort and safety.

We are indeed very fortunate that we no longer have the military draft that was such a defining feature of previous generations. Our current all-volunteer military means that today's young people grow up without knowledge of or experience with what registering for the draft entails. They don't understand the weight of that eighteen-year-old milestone when young men had to report to their local draft board and face the very real possibility of being called to serve, whether they felt ready or not.

But I believe strongly that they should learn about this history and understand these realities. They should know that, while we hope and pray it never becomes necessary, the draft could still be reinstated if our nation faces an existential threat. We don't hope for such circumstances, but if we truly want to preserve our freedoms and way of life for future generations, we need robust, capable armed forces. And that means having citizens who understand their potential obligations and responsibilities to their country, even in times when such service is not actively required. This understanding creates better citizens and ensures that our democracy remains strong and our freedoms remain secure.

CHAPTER 22

After Retirement Travels

* * *

Trips Through Europe – 1997

In 1997, Martha and I went to Holland to attend my mother's family reunion. As always, it was an emotional experience to see my mother and reconnect with my siblings and extended family. The warmth of that gathering, with its mixture of laughter, tears, and shared memories, reminded us of the irreplaceable bonds of family. After spending a few cherished days in Holland, we rented a car and drove to Italy, where we visited the town of Assisi, home of Saint Francis. We also visited the city of Padua and San Giovanni Rotondo, a town in the province of Foggia in southern Italy, where Padre Pio is buried.

The absolute highlight of our visit to Rome came during our time at the Vatican. We attended the Wednesday papal audience, followed by Holy Mass, which the Holy Father, Pope John Paul II, celebrated. We had front-row seats, and it was a marvel to watch the Mass from up front. After the Mass, the Holy Father, as was his custom, rode in his popemobile to greet and shake hands with many of the attendees, especially those seated at the front. He passed just inches away from where we stood in the crowd. In fact, Martha stretched out her hand and nearly touched his as he passed by, while I stood just a few feet behind, trying to capture the moment on camera. It was a truly transcendent moment for us—one of those rare instances when faith becomes tangible and unforgettable. This feeling intensified when we visited the Sistine Chapel, and I was able to climb into the dome of Saint Peter's Basilica - truly amazing!

We spent another week relaxing along the Adriatic coast, enjoying the sun, sea, and stunning coastal scenery. Finally, we made our way back to Holland, taking a scenic route through the majestic Swiss Alps and the charming countryside of Germany.

Trip to Honolulu, Hawaii, 1997

We also traveled to Honolulu, Hawaii, where we visited the solemn and powerful USS Arizona Memorial at Pearl Harbor. This moving memorial commemorates the Japanese attack on the United States that drew America into World War II—a day that, as President Roosevelt declared, would "live in infamy."

The USS Arizona was a U.S. Navy battleship tragically sunk during the surprise attack on Pearl Harbor on December 7, 1941. Of the 1,177 crew members who perished in the attack, 1,102 remain entombed within the ship's submerged hull, which still rests on the harbor floor. The memorial, a stark white structure built directly over the sunken battleship, serves as both a tomb and a tribute to those who made the ultimate sacrifice.

Standing above the wreckage and looking down at the rusting hull visible beneath the clear water was profoundly emotional. Oil still seeps from the ship—what some call "the tears of the Arizona"—serving as a constant reminder of that fateful day. We also explored the Pearl Harbor Visitor Center and museum, where exhibits, artifacts, and personal stories brought the events of December 7, 1941, vividly to life and deepened our understanding of this pivotal moment in American history.

Travel to the Holy Land 1998

Our pilgrimage to the Holy Land in 1998 was a very special trip for Martha and me. We were still living in Templeton when we joined a group of pilgrims—about twenty people in all—traveling to this sacred destination. The ten-day journey was a beautiful experience.

As often happens in our area, parishes organize pilgrimages to holy sites around the world, particularly to the Holy Land. We joined one such organized trip and were not disappointed in the slightest. Aptly called "In the Footsteps of Jesus," the pilgrimage took us to Bethlehem, Nazareth, Jerusalem—all the places we had longed to see.

We flew into Tel Aviv and, to our great surprise, caught a glimpse of Israeli Prime Minister Benjamin Netanyahu as he was entering the same hotel we were staying at. We could barely see him, though, because he was heavily surrounded by his security detail.

One of the most moving experiences during our trip was being baptized by immersion in the Jordan River. It wasn't a sacramental baptism because we didn't need to be baptized again. Rather, it was a symbolic reenactment of John the Baptist's baptism of Jesus. The experience was quite powerful and deeply meaningful.

We also renewed our wedding vows in Cana, the very place where Christ performed His first miracle, changing water into wine during a wedding feast. The ceremony added a special dimension to our own marriage as we stood where that ancient celebration had taken place.

Another highlight was ascending Mount Tabor, the Mount of the Transfiguration, where Jesus was transfigured before Peter, James, and John. The views from the summit were breathtaking, and standing on that holy ground brought the Gospel accounts vividly to life.

Trip to Paris – 2000

In the year 2000, we took a memorable five-day trip to Paris. We did considerable touring in and around the city, visiting iconic landmarks such as the Eiffel Tower, the Louvre Museum, and several magnificent cathedrals. We admired Notre Dame Cathedral, viewing its Gothic splendor from the outside, and visited the Basilica of the Sacred Heart (Sacré-Cœur) perched atop Montmartre, among other sites. We traveled throughout Paris by metro and bus, immersing ourselves in the rhythm of the city, and enjoyed lunch and dinner at some excellent restaurants that gave us an authentic taste of French cuisine.

After five enriching days in Paris, we rented a car and drove to Holland, where we spent a week with my family. It was another wonderful reunion after many years apart.

Trip to China – 2000

The trip to China was also an amazing adventure. We spent four days in Beijing as part of a comprehensive three-week journey that took us across much of the country. The trip was organized by a Chinese travel agency based in San Francisco, and we traveled with a group of about forty Americans.

We visited the Forbidden City, the Temple of Heaven, and the Great Wall of China. Walking along its ancient ramparts, we marveled at this extraordinary feat of human engineering, stretching across mountains and valleys. We explored Tiananmen Square, one of the world's largest public squares, and visited numerous scenic and historic sites throughout the country. In Beijing, visibility was limited because the air was thick with dust from a large desert sandstorm.

Communication was not a problem, as our tour guides were Chinese who spoke perfect English. Most of the food was unfamiliar but very tasty. Some members of our group were unable to eat many of the dishes because they did not know what they were. As for me, I liked all their food. We were, however, surprised by all the modern buildings, highways, and bridges, as well as by the numerous construction sites where tall buildings were being built using bamboo scaffolding.

Our journey took us by various means of transportation—train, bus, and plane—as we crisscrossed China, each mode offering a unique perspective on the vast and diverse landscape. From bustling modern cities to serene rural areas, from ancient temples to contemporary landmarks, the trip gave us a comprehensive view of China's rich culture, long history, and rapid development.

One of the most spectacular highlights was our cruise on the Yangtze River. This was before the construction of the Three

Gorges Dam, so we were fortunate to experience the river in its original, natural state—a privilege that few travelers today can claim. The dramatic gorges, towering cliffs, and ancient riverside villages created a truly breathtaking and unforgettable scene.

Trip to Egypt 2004

In 2004, we visited Egypt, which turned out to be another incredible experience. We took a cruise on the Nile River—an absolutely awe-inspiring journey, which took us all the way up to the Aswan Dam. We sailed past the pyramids and numerous burial sites of the ancient pharaohs in the Valley of the Kings. The climate there is extraordinarily dry, which explains why so many mummified pharaohs have been well preserved over the millennia.

While we were unable to enter the largest pyramids, we did have the opportunity to explore some of the smaller ones. Along the Nile, we encountered countless temples, and it was simply amazing to see how well-preserved some of these structures remain, even after thousands of years.

We also visited the Egyptian Museum in Cairo, where I was most impressed with the gold artifacts. One of my favorite places was the world's oldest library in Alexandria, where I was able to use a computer and send an email to a family member back home. It was then rebuilt, as the original was destroyed by fire. Martha bought new eyeglasses made in Cairo, which were comparatively very cheap.

Latin American Trips

We took trips to Costa Rica and the Dominican Republic, both of which were fantastic experiences. We also visited Martha's home country of El Salvador, where she hadn't been in quite some time. It was a meaningful journey—we were able to spend time with her family and also meet a child we were sponsoring through a charitable organization.

The boy lived in El Salvador and was attending a school run by nuns. We called ahead to ask if we could visit him, and they warmly welcomed us. They even sent a car to pick us up at the airport at five o'clock in the morning. We were delighted to meet the child and see the tremendous progress he was making in his studies. We ended up spending five days with the nuns—a stay we truly appreciated and cherished.

Afterward, we visited Martha's family—this was the third time I had visited them since our marriage. Martha comes from a city called Santa Tecla, located several miles outside the capital, San Salvador. My fourth and final visit to El Salvador was a somber one: we brought Martha's mother's mortal remains back home for burial.

Trip to Thailand – 2005

In 2005, we took a trip to Thailand that turned out to be truly extraordinary. We visited Bangkok, of course, with its bustling streets and vibrant culture. From there, we took a bus journey to several cities north of the capital, and this proved to be a fabulous adventure in itself.

Our guide was a woman with encyclopedic knowledge of the places we visited. She spoke beautiful, fluent English and graciously invited us to her father's farm, where she gave us a hands-on demonstration of how to plow a rice paddy. To our amazement, she did it herself right there before our eyes, guiding the plow through the flooded field with practiced skill.

We also had the unforgettable opportunity to ride one of the enormous water buffaloes so common throughout Thailand. Sitting atop these gentle giants was both thrilling and humbling—an experience we'll never forget. We also rode an elephant and visited an elephant hospital where elephants that were wounded mainly by land mines that are still found in many areas in that region of the world, especially in Burma.

As we traveled from one city to another, from one village to the next, we immersed ourselves in Thai culture and spirituality. We visited numerous Buddhist temples, their golden spires glinting in the tropical sun, and participated in the traditional morning ritual of bringing food to the monks. Offering alms at dawn, as the saffron-robed monks walked in silent procession, was a profoundly moving experience that gave us insight into the deep spirituality that permeates daily life in Thailand.

The Thai people seem very industrious; many were artisans who created beautiful handmade items. We attended a cooking class, and I made a Thai meal. We also visited the floating markets and a flower market, which was of great interest to me.

We walked across the bridge over the River Kuai. I had read the book about it and seen the movie of that title several years ago. We also visited the cemetery, where more than 3,000 Royal Dutch Army and Navy personnel are buried. They had died as prisoners of war while constructing the Burma railway and during the infamous "dead march."

Trip to Russia 2008

We visited Russia in 2008 on an extraordinary overland journey that began in Copenhagen. Traveling by bus, we passed through Denmark, Sweden, and Finland before arriving in St. Petersburg, and then continued to Moscow, where we explored Red Square and other historic sites. We were not allowed inside the Kremlin. We did not see the GUM department store either, but we did see Saint Basil's Cathedral on Red Square. The Moscow deep underground station was very impressive. We admired its beautiful architecture with great pillars and stained-glass windows. For the tourists, some people in the street were dressed as Lenin and Stalin. In Saint Petersburg, we saw much more, including the beautiful music hall where we watched Russian operas and plays. In the harbor of Saint Petersburg, we visited a Russian battleship, where I touched the cannon that fired the first shot that started the Bolshevik Revolution on October 25, 1917. That was the revolution led by Vladimir Lenin and the Bolshevik Party, that overthrew the Provisional Government and established a communist government, marking the beginning of Soviet rule in Russia. That made a big impression on me.

From Russia, we traveled to Belarus and then on to Poland, where we visited Wadowice, the birthplace of Pope John Paul II.

Our journey also included visits to the infamous concentration camps. It was a profoundly sobering experience to witness firsthand the places where humanity's inhumanity to humankind was so horrifically displayed under Adolf Hitler. We concluded our European tour in Berlin, Germany, and then flew back to San Francisco.

European River Cruise

We returned to Europe in 2012. Beginning in Prague, where we spent three memorable days, we traveled by bus to Budapest. There, we embarked on one of the long ships down the Danube and Rhine rivers—quite an amazing journey through the heart of Europe, with a final destination in Amsterdam.

Trips in the United States 2019

At one point, we realized that while we had cruised some of the world-renowned rivers, such as the Yangtze in China, the Nile in Egypt and the Rhine and Danube in Europe, we had not yet explored our own rivers in the United States. That is why we decided to remedy this by taking a steamboat down the Mississippi River. We traveled from Memphis, Tennessee, to New Orleans, stopping at various fascinating cities along the way.

In the Footsteps of the Apostle Paul 2021

The last major trip we took before the COVID-19 pandemic brought international travel to a halt was a pilgrimage to Greece and Turkey, organized by Mike Huckabee, former governor of Arkansas and a well-known Christian leader. He accompanied us on the journey, and I had the pleasure of chatting with him on several occasions during the trip. He struck me as a very pleasant individual—open, personable, and genuinely interested in listening to others. He later became the United States Ambassador to Israel under President Donald Trump.

The pilgrimage was called "Walking in the Footsteps of the Apostle Paul," and we visited many of the cities where the Apostle Paul once preached. To say it was an exciting trip would be an understatement—we thoroughly enjoyed every moment. While in Turkey, we took an unforgettable hot air balloon ride, and the scenery from above was truly breathtaking.

In Greece, we visited several islands and locations mentioned in the Bible where Saint Paul preached the Gospel, including Santorini, the Areopagus in Athens, and other significant sites. From Athens, we sailed to Istanbul and then returned home to San Francisco.

Back to Holland 2023

My trips to Holland were mostly to visit my family, and typically only on special occasions such as anniversaries and milestone celebrations. On my brother Teun's 40th wedding anniversary, I decided to surprise them with an unexpected visit. They had absolutely no idea I was coming. I conspired with their children to hide me inside a large television box, which they placed at the front door. They rang the bell and quickly disappeared. When my brother and his wife came outside, they were puzzled to find the enormous box on their doorstep. I could hear them talking and wondering what could possibly be inside. The moment they opened it, I sprang out shouting, "Surprise!" They were utterly shocked—none of them had the slightest clue I would be coming. We had a beautiful time together as a family.

There were also somber occasions for additional visits, the last days of my parents, my brother and my sister. I was able to visit each of them shortly before they died. Even though I was not able to be present for any of their funerals, I was at peace and honored to have visited all of them just weeks before they died. My mother passed away first at the age of 84, and my father followed not long afterward at the age of 86. One of my last visits was for my brother Jan's birthday, a month before he passed away.

I returned to Holland at the end of September 2024 for my school reunion, celebrating 150 years of the school's existence. Everyone who had ever attended the school was invited.

I decided it was an excellent opportunity to attend, but until three days before the event, my doctor had not yet given me medical clearance to travel. However, he finally granted his permission when my oldest daughter, Betsy, a registered nurse, agreed to accompany me. So off I went, hoping to reconnect with old classmates, exchange memories, and learn how everyone was faring after all these years.

It turned out, however, that only two of us from my class were present—and we were the oldest people among all 750 attendees. The rest of my classmates had either already passed away or were too ill to attend. It was a bittersweet moment, a poignant reminder of the passage of time.

Visit to the Vatican in 1997. Martha stretching out her hand to greet
Pope John Paul II in Saint Peter's Square.

Visiting the pyramids of Egypt in 2004

Visitng Tianamen Square in Beijing, China, in 2000

Riding an elephant in Thailand in
2005

Visiting Red Square in Moscow in 2008

Martha and I at the foot
of the Christ Statue in
Havana, Cuba

Visiting a school in Uganda in 2009

Learning to play the drum; Uganda, 2009

Thank you, America

* * *

America, you were not merely a destination when I arrived in California in 1957—you were a resurrection. Where Europe had offered me the ruins of a shattered world, you offered me open skies, fertile land, and the radical promise that a man's future was his own to build. Every sunrise in California was a gift that millions of others never received, and I carried that knowledge with me every single day of my life.

That gratitude was never passive, America! It blossomed into an extraordinary life of creation and contribution. You gave me land, freedom, and dignity, and I repaid you with the full measure of my labor and ingenuity.

My story is a testament to what you, America, have always meant to those who arrive on your shores fleeing darkness: not just a place to live, but a reason to live — and a calling to give back everything, and then some. This is why I tell my story:

to share what I have learned and experienced through many changes in my life, from where my journey began so long ago.

America, Land of the Free! I will always hold my birth country close to my heart, but today I am a proud American, eternally grateful. You embraced me with open arms, allowing me to build a new life and to meet Martha — the love of my life, the heart of our family, and the mother of our children.

America, Land of the Brave! Thank you for your unwavering commitment to freedom and your tireless efforts to defend liberty around the world. Your courage and resolve continue to inspire and uplift all who seek peace, justice, and opportunity.

* * *

Note: In January 2014, I participated in a recorded personal narrative video for the Veterans History Project. The video is accessible by visiting the following Library of Congress website link: https://www.loc.gov/item/afc2001001.95994/

About the author

Henry A. Mulder was born in 1937 in the Netherlands and emigrated to California in 1957. A horticultural pioneer, he co-founded a floral business that thrived for four decades and was twice named "Farmer of the Year." His life has been defined by a deep commitment to service—from his years as a medical corpsman in the National Guard to his volunteer work at Ground Zero in New York City following the September 11, 2001, terrorist attacks on the Twin Towers. Henry and his wife, Martha, raised six children together, passing down values of gratitude, hard work, and family that continue to thrive across generations.

About the Publisher

Maple Books is an imprint of Spears Media Press LLC dedicated to publishing diverse, high-quality narratives that transcend borders and genres; our mission is to partner with authors from all walks of life to transform their unique insights into professionally crafted books that inform, entertain, and inspire—reaching a truly global audience. We believe in bridging the gap between inspired manuscripts and the worldwide marketplace of ideas.

Learn more at www.spearsbooks.org.

www.ingramcontent.com/pod-product-compliance
Lightning Source LLC
Chambersburg PA
CBHW022050050726

47591CB00002B/476